The High Life

From the 60's to Being Sixty

By
ROGER E. PROULX

The High Life: From the 60's to Being Sixty

Published by *Double R Concepts,*
Tampa Bay, Florida

Copyright © 2010 by Roger E. Proulx, Author
ISBN: 978-0-578-06307-2

Printed in the United States of America

CONTENTS

DEDICATION

I dedicate the success and enjoyment of creating the following stories to my parents, in appreciation of their enduring patience, the dynamic harmony they taught their children to embrace, and their limitless power to love all of us.

INTRODUCTION

When I was first born, I was born first of all my siblings. I had loving people all around me, fighting to hold me, make me smile or utter a noise. Anything I did would rouse my fan club to gushing praises. My parents really deserved all the credit. Not only did they provide the genetics and all the gear, but the cause of all this special adoration was that they were so well loved by their families and friends, that it just rubbed off onto me...my true inheritance. It didn't hurt that I was the first born grandchild on my father's side, or that I was a boy: something that cannot be openly defended in our times. But in those times, they were customary beliefs among my grandparents, who were born in the 19th Century. In their eyes, I was something akin to the "future patriarch," the first edition of the new family branch, and the coming, big fish of the expanding gene pool.

Then, I'm told, I became a "colicky baby," stricken with stomach cramps. As the condition continued, I became a scourge upon my parents as they struggled in vain to relieve my pains. This changed the warm glow of a full house of laughing kin into empty rooms filled with ear piercing, brain jamming noises as I cried out for many days and nights. Those who were chosen to be special to me, such as my Godparents probably wanted to void their contracts. My Godfather, Uncle Moe, declared his allegiance, but felt compelled to tell my mother I was "...the ugliest baby I have ever seen...his head is shaped like a rocket."

iii

It also became a gut check ordeal for my grandparents, as a colicky baby constantly needs attention to be soothed. So when my once proud and happy parents became burnt out and sleep deprived, they looked to *their* parents as the first line of support and back-up for their poor baby's needs. I needed this net to give me a chance of surviving until I righted myself. I was lucky to have had that core support. True, some relatives were less enthusiastic and secretly complained if asked to walk me around, or even be in the same house, subjected to my screaming. But fearing the wrath of my grandparents, none would bring it up, or fail to help out. If it was casually mentioned, an hour could be spent re-hashing how absolutely horrible I was: a cranky baby: the atom bomb of babies. I left scars that remain to this day with the survivors of my short-lived role as #1 baby.

At only a couple months old, I must have instinctively knew the trouble I was in and of my fall from grace. So after some genius figured out I was allergic to orange juice, I instantly shut up and learned to walk by the time I was eight months old. This feat put me back on the "A' list" of family babies that were now popping out everywhere. I sprouted a quick first tooth, another positive conversation topic. Still, my place in the spotlight was doomed, as my mother soon became pregnant and delivered another baby boy before I even had a full year in the spotlight. I couldn't know this was only the beginning; just the start of my parents' New Baby Parade that would roll on for a decade of uniquely cute and prettier babies each year, none with colic.

Then we generated our own baby parades

and multiple generations who all carry a number of common traits with the original producers.

These stories are an attempt to get the attention of all my relatives back on me.

SEX TUNNELS OF HAZARDVILLE

The leader scanned his noisy young comrades, and began to order them to positions along the dirt road when their talking instantly stopped; bodies froze in motion, and tanned faces turned pale, their eyes staring past him. In a single moment, the troop scattered in all directions of the surrounding thicket. For a few seconds, Jack stood still, staring at the now empty log his brotherhood had just filled as a shared seat. He wondered what could cause his Blackhawks, his seasoned woodland warriors, to bolt. Never before had they fled a fight or animal attack, nature's dangers or developers' bulldozers.

He gave the secret Blackhawk call for them. There was no response, but he did hear noise in the bushes and instinctively crouched down while slowly turning in the direction of the street. Half-way around, he saw Rozzy and Jenny wearing only beach towels, jumping, each waving one arm while the other held up their towel, "Watch out! Watch out!" they screamed, pointing to his left. He turned to see a small blond woman several yards away, running straight at him, swinging a razor strap. With each stride, a smoking cigarette bounced between her painted, red lips, her blond ponytail popped up and down above her enraged face as she bellowed curses.

"You little shit asses, little fuckers! I'm gonna strap your balls 'till they bleed!"

"Nice mother, good citizen..." Jack thought. With her red fingernails, swim top, and Keds setting off her white short-shorts, she appeared to be a wheel of red and white -hot flame roaring straight at his stiff, planted body.

Something in Jack told him not to pivot and run straight for the woods. Instead, he quickly faked running to his right, toward the street. The smoking blond literally fell for this move, landing in some low raspberry bushes, and giving Jack just enough time to turn and run to the

2

smooth dirt road he had just traveled. She stumbled while changing direction in the snagging bushes. Jack was now a fast runner with a slight lead on a madwoman with skinned knees. He had to increase his lead, tiring her out with a fast pace, then turn off the road into the cover of the woods and lose her.

He felt his heart pumping in his head, his feet hitting the road, pushing back dirt, and the wind rushing over his crew cut. Jack wondered why this woman was chasing them down...well, just him right now. Her chase deeply pissed him off. He figured if she was somebody's mother and knew about the plan, she should have called their parents and not let Rozzy and Jen come out here at all. This person let us come to the meet-up so she could trap one of us... and let the brass-hooked strap sings its song.

Glancing over his shoulder, he was baffled to see she was on pace with him. He was certain his mother couldn't run like that. This she- devil was in good physical shape and driven by rage. She must be Rozzy's mom. Rozzy had told him her mom used a razor strap to hit her anytime she goofed up. Sometimes she'd get strapped for no reason other than her mother had a few drinks. Mother wasn't drunk now. Maybe she was popping diet pills. Jack began to reckon this child beater might be able to stay close or even catch up to him on this straight track. So he decided to leave the road sooner for an area he knew would be marshy, but one he could log jump faster than she would.

This maneuver slowed her enough for Jack to get out of easy sight. But he kept going as fast as he could, reaching the wood's end, where he dove over a wall of shiny rubbish cans at the back of someone's yard. Jack took a crouched position behind the cans, peering through the spaces between them toward the marsh

3

area. He watched and listened for her approach.

Nothing snapping or cursing. He finally had a chance to think about what had just happened. One minute he was about to safely rendezvous with a neighborhood girl wearing only a towel—the next, she and his loyal buddies were scattered across the woods and he was running for his life from a howling banshee dressed as a pool mom. He couldn't believe how easily this person was able to sneak up on them, charge them into a panic and destroy their plan. They prided themselves on being experienced swampers and woodsmen who snuck up on other people.

Maybe it was the Hazardville Curse. Plans had a way of going wrong in Hazardville, he sulked. As much as he loved the freedom of the forest that fronted the tobacco field, Jack Prowse wondered why his parents decided to move here, leaving the comforts of the city: movie theaters in walking distance; buses stopping at your front door, ready to take you to parks, department stores, and zoos. His parents always talked about missing their family and friends, and something they called the swing of city life. So, why'd they leave to come here?

Ed and Betty Prowse had to get out of Dodge. Not for a long weekend at a seaside resort on Cape Cod... but actually get out of Pawtucket, Rhode Island. They were not going away to escape creditors, or to elude the FBI, DEA, CIA or the Mafia. They had to leave to save their sanity from their three sons, ages 4, 3, and 2 who were going nuts and taking Ed and Betty with them. Living on the third floor of a tenement in urban Rhode Island at a time when TV was a test pattern for most of the daytime-- broadcast on your choice of three channels--with no play yard and only Gramma Beaulieu to amuse and contain them, the boys were taking jumps from the food cabinet to the kitchen table, falling down flights of stairs, and hanging off the third-floor balcony. Ed and Betty needed a safer and larger place to bring up the 'monstas'. They went to Hazardville, Connecticut. The town name translated to: Village of Danger beside the Long Tidal River.

If they had checked around a bit, they might have learned the village was sitting on an actual giant powder keg, a crater-like hollow, probably formed by a crashing meteorite: the Powder Hollow Bowl. It was 150 feet deep, over a mile in diameter and was the largest source of gun powder production for the United States military during the Spanish-American and American Civil War. During the eighty-odd years the powder mill operated, sixty-seven men were killed at work, despite extreme precautions [like one-legged stools and double thick walls] to avoid and contain blasts. The Blast of 1917, one of several big ones, finally closed the mill. Canisters and barrels of gunpowder exploded while others flew through the air. Dry powder kegs continued to be found within the Hollow for decades.

The village's natural surroundings were surely beautiful, with many fiery sugar maples and evergreens, rolling hills, and peaceful breezes. All this precariously bordered on one side by the long, deep and dangerous Connecticut River, which would sometimes overflow its banks; and a rocky, smaller river, filled with shad for fishing, many rapids, whirlpools, and deep holes named the Scitico River. If you were fortunate enough to avoid being blown up or drowned, the many fields around the village were growing poisonous tobacco plants and eight-foot King snakes, that ate the local rattlesnakes that ate the many large and small rodents that loved life in the endless rows of tobacco plants. Several icons of Man's most dreaded industrial, health, and natural perils were brought together in one, little village.

Yet, they named it not for these dangers, but because the man who brought it national commerce was named Hazard, Augustus Hazard. He was the most successful of several owners of the gun powder mill, expanding it to fifty buildings and twenty-five water wheels. Despite his wealth, Hazard was not entirely successful. One of his two sons died in an explosion. Did Augustus magnify the hazard in Hazardville, or were there already hazards enough for this village's namesake? In both ways, hazardous was an apt description of the village's natural and economic history.

But people didn't vet things like they do today. For a baby-making machine like the Prowse's, who were averaging one child per year practicing the Church's rhythm method of birth control, Hazardville was a nice fit. It had plenty of fresh air and space for their future surprises. What they couldn't foresee was that their offspring would become another hazard in Hazardville. The simple fact was that Ed didn't have much time to find their future home. He went to see the place only once and chose it because it was near his new job. He used his G.I. Bill to quickly secure a mortgage, then went back for the family and a moving truck.

Whatever the reasons that caused him to be here, they were in the past. Jack had a problem in the present moment. He quickly resumed listening and watching. So far, the only sounds were from the middle of the marsh. Soon, he heard the "thuck" of her steps and the "fuck!" in her shouts. She was wandering in the mire, but getting closer to the wood's end somewhere to his right.

Then he heard a familiar sound from behind him: the lever action of a BB rifle being cocked. "What are you doin' in my yard, ass-wipe?" It was the voice of his arch enemy, Billy Fuller. He pointed the rifle at Jack's face. "Runnin' away from Rozzy's cute, crazy mommy?"

"Your trash barrels smell like shit, Fuller. You still crapping your undies and throwing 'em out in the rubbish?"

Billy glared at him.

"Hey! Mrs. Corsa! He's over here!" cried Billy.

He turned from Jack to wave her over to the cans. Jack knew this was his best chance to slip the BB pistol out from the back of his belt. He raised the pistol and aimed at Fuller's chest as he turned back to face him. But Fuller started ducking when he spotted the pistol, causing Jack's shot to hit his ear lobe, splitting it. This was great luck for Jack, because ear lobes easily bleed a lot. Blood started to run down the hand he put over his ear, and he yelled for help while Jack grabbed the rifle and took off. Michelle Corsa quickly arrived at the spot, only to get caught up in helping Mrs. Fuller attend to her wounded son.

Jack reached the cover of the tobacco field. He ducked in a few yards and squatted silently among the tall plants, looking out toward the road and the path for the she-devil. He waited and listened, but there was no sign of a chaser. Jack decided to move out toward the main fort and try to meet up with his brothers and any other Hawks who may have hid out there.

He hoped they didn't run straight home or get too spread out after their panic. He trained them to stay in pairs and regain calm after a sudden attack. The fort was not far. Staying low, Jack took a couple of quick steps across the rows before he tripped over a small log. He sat up and kicked it. But it wasn't a small log, it slowly turned toward him: a large, black King Snake, with white rings around its thick, smooth body. Yellow eyes glowed in its

V-shaped head, and a long, flicking tongue constantly shot from its mouth. Their eyes met and locked on each other, watching for any movement. He had killed this kind of snake before; but with a strong wooden spear, two other Hawks to surround the snake, and while standing up at a longer distance than the few feet between them now.

Keeping steady eye contact with the snake, Jack remembered the last time he saw one it was loosely curled in a shallow pit. Around the snake sat his little brothers and sisters, quietly watching it. His siblings were never as quiet as they were at that moment, like they were mesmerized by the big snake's restful gaze. His sisters should have been screaming, his brothers launching spears and stones at the serpent. Instead they just watched, feeling as secure as the snake seemed to be. Jack hated to call them in for supper. When he silently motioned them to head in, they looked at him like, "Can the snake come, too?" The snake stayed right where he was, but he never saw it there again.

"Raaaahzeeeee! Raaaahzeeeee! Mrs. Corsa's search call pierced the silence like the screech of a bird of prey. The large snake felt the vibrations of these screams and zigged off, as fast as its belly could carry it, toward the woods. Jack stayed low, pistol and rifle ready, his hatchet in hand. He was determined this charged- up woman wasn't gonna take his eye out with the brass end of a razor strap...not without suffering some damage to her body.

Then the snake appeared again -- crossing the path not ten feet in front of the she-devil, who had sucked in a belly full of wind to blow out another search cry. The sight of a fast-winding, eight foot serpent flashing into her vision twisted her yell into an incomprehensible wail of horror enough to wake the dead. She impulsively

8

threw the strap toward the moving snake, then sprinted back the way she came, toward the safety of paved streets and fenced yards. Jack wanted to enjoy a good laugh, but instead ran out to grab the strap.

"She has one less weapon. And I might need it as evidence she came prepared to wail on us," he reasoned.

It was time to move quickly to the main fort and check for his comrades. Approaching the fort, he silently crawled to the underground door and slowly entered--no one home. The pump BB rifle and all the spears were there, fireworks, too. Jack grabbed a spear and the flashlight after hiding the strap and Fuller's BB rifle. He flashed the light down all three tunnels--nothing. Where were they? In an emergency, the standing order was to meet up at the tree fort. Adults couldn't climb the tree [even if they found it] and it provided a wide field of vision and hearing of the ground below.

On the way, Jack wanted to look around the smaller fort and carefully poke his head out for a scan of the wagon lane. If they were still there, he didn't want to leave them behind with the she-devil in the area. Jack decided to carefully walk along the edge of the road up to the tunnel "drop door", then get down in and crawl, unseen, to the other end of the road. He saw no one. He heard only the familiar sounds of the woods. It appeared that the brothers were hiding out, captured, or retreated to their homes. Jack felt concerned and abandoned.

It was only yesterday that the gang was in high spirits, eager to hear about an offer from Rozzy and her cousin, Jenny, to be taken blindfolded and naked under towels to the Tunnel Fort in exchange for a tour of their tunnels. Jack and Kevin thought it was a joke, but wanted to plan it out, in case Rozzy was serious.

They gathered deep in the woods, on the spine of the forest floor-- a narrow strip of earth and stone that divided a quietly menacing swamp supporting the life and death of the predator and the prey: hawks diving for snakes, snakes digesting frogs; frogs munching bugs; bugs biting kids, kids biting kids; an authentic reality show called the "food chain." Plant life was everywhere in, around and over the black water, reducing the noonday's sun to fragile rays that barely reached the slippery passageway. Further along, it widened into a wagon lane connecting this minestrone bio-soup on the edge of Hazardville's tobacco fields to the nicely uniform, dry, asphalt streets of the housing plats, schools, stores, and soda shops.

The Blackhawks, as they called themselves, reveled in this swampy woodland beyond their backyards. The gang was an alliance of groups of brothers living on the same street. They adopted the name "Blackhawks" from the comic book heroes, imaginary Allied fighter pilots, heroes of WWII who battled the Nazis for control of the European sky. The boys only wanted to keep control of the swamp, but identified with the Blackhawks because they were warriors from different countries who put their differences aside to fight as one unit. The brother groups were also from different ethnic backgrounds: Italian, Finnish, French, Scottish, Polish; also fighting one enemy— the land developer. The Blackhawk squadron uniform: black leather coat and boots, silk ascot, a rakish aviator cap, and some unique symbol of their nationality had a certain appeal to them; and "Blackhawk" just sounded cool, and still does, especially for anything used in aerial combat.

The muddy hideaway was diverse and isolated enough for them to get away with messing with the scenery: building dams to form ponds, cutting paths through the undergrowth, digging up bushes, riding trees

10

to the ground, hunting and capturing whatever they could, and constructing forts, rafts, and a maze of tunnels. The forgotten forest and swamp land was their rent-free acting studio, nature laboratory, and secret retreat. Though young, they would use all their strength and imagination to preserve it.

On this day in early September, The Blackhawks attention was fixed on Jack, who led them out of the swamp toward the Wilderness Road. Speaking quietly, he pointed to different positions along the way. Now and then, he stopped speaking and looked directly into the face of a member before giving him instructions for his part in the overall plan. The Blackhawks were preparing for authentic action. Having grown up watching war films, Westerns, and monster movies, they were always ready for the chance to act-out armed combat at any level of competition. But meeting girls in the woods was unknown territory, so it deserved more preparation than a typical BB gun fight.

After everyone was given their assignment, the group started to joke around and relax from paying more attention than they ever did in school. After a few minutes, the leader quieted them with his raised arm. For just a moment he turned his back to the other Blackhawks, carefully choosing those points he most wanted them to remember. He adjusted his two belts, a sheathed hunting knife on his pants belt and a hatchet strapped with rawhide to his free belt. Jack's lean, serious face looked older than most pre-teens, and bore a slightly crescent-shaped scar from the corner of his right eye down to the cheekbone. He didn't get the scar in a fight, but from his justly annoyed Aunt Isabel's flying spatula. This was Hazardville and hazards were plentiful; some natural, and some man-made. He turned to the party.

"Remember, we meet here tomorrow, right after

lunch. Then each of you will take his look-out place on the road or on the trail to the fort. Kevin and I will meet the "towel girls" at the other end of the road at 1 p.m. ... if they show. As we take them toward the fort," he looked at Cary and Bobby, "You two follow us from a distance, watching behind for any followers. The rest of you stay in your position for a few minutes, and then follow us.

For now, we have to clean the fort and the tunnels. Get rid of any junk, stones, and bugs. Girls hate bugs. And they're not going to want to take their towels off in a place they don't feel is safe and clean. I'm pretty sure of that."

One of the younger Hawks approached the leader, who was also his older brother.

"I know I kinda asked you about this before, Jack, but are we gonna get in real trouble if we get caught doin' this?" Keith sputtered, nervously.

"First, we're not getting caught if you follow orders. Remember, no one knows where our fort is except us. So we can't be found if you don't get followed. And second, the girls are gonna be blindfolded so they won't be able to say where they went--unless one of you blabs", Jack stressed as he again looked at each member of the group, "Even if we do get caught, we'll just tell 'em the truth: we found the girls breakin' in to one of our forts. They asked us if they could stay if they took their clothes off, but we said, 'No." Then they dared us to let them come another day, wearing only towels. This is their idea. They dared us. We're not making them do anything. Now, let's get cleaning."

Once they reached the main fort, the hub of the three tunnels, Keith, began acting strangely nervous. Jack looked over at him and then motioned Keith to follow

12

him into the fort, while the others continued to spruce up the tunnel area. Once inside, Jack looked his brother over for any outward signs of distress, like a cut, bruise, or missing shoe.

"You don't look so good, Keith. You OK? Are you thirsty, or need to go to the bathroom?" Jack asked, knowing the usual causes of distress to his shy, younger brother. Keith shook his head side-to-side, looking at the ground. "What's wrong? Are you getting scared about Rozzy and her friend coming here?"

"Well, I'm not afraid of them, exactly. I just don't ...I don't want to see bare girls", Keith struggled to explain, "I feel like if I look at them, then they'll want me to say something to them or do something back, and I don't know what to do. I don't want to do anything...even look."

Jack laughed to himself at how shook up Keith was at the prospect of seeing bare girls. Not that seeing bare girls was an everyday event, it amused Jack that the little guy doesn't hesitate to ride a 30 ft. tree to the ground, or stab a large King Snake with a wooden spear. But a fear is a fear, and it doesn't have to be rational, necessary, or consistent with other behavior.

"Don't worry, Keith," Jack assured him," "They're probably not gonna show. And if they do, they won't be naked...just towels wrapped around their clothes to trick us. Maybe she wants to get something on us that she can tell her parents and get us in trouble. Well, we have a surprise for her and her friend.

We will bring them here, and show 'em into the tunnels for a while. Then, at the right moment, we'll split from them into one of the side-tunnels, leaving them in the dark with no idea how to find their way around. By the time they find their way out, their parents will be worried but pissed at them when they finally get home for staying outside so late. We'll be home watching television."

"Ok, then," said Keith, "It's much better if it works out that way, 'cuz if Rozzy keeps following us she'll get bare one time when we're not looking and then we'll see her by surprise, unless we plan it first."

"Yeah... you got it, Henderson [Keith's code name among the Blackhawks]"

Having settled that matter, the brothers joined the others at work on the tunnels that connected their three forts. These tunnels were narrow, three to four foot deep trenches. Most were 20-30 feet long, shoveled out of the soft, clay-like soil of the woods nearest the tobacco fields. The trenches were hidden by a "cover" of small logs, branches, and planks. Built by 10 to twelve year olds, the tunnels were hardly "up to code". The sides could cave in, and someone might easily step through the top covering. The bottom would sometimes become a home for rodents, spiders, and snakes. These camouflaged, quickly made tunnel covers and forts were punctuated by rusty nails and sharp, branch stubs. Proudly "Made in Hazardville, U.S.A.," by the Blackhawks.

All this digging, banging, and chopping did not go un-noticed, but it didn't cause real concern for their equally delusional parents. The nearby woods didn't look too deep to them. Nor was it really a secret to their mothers, who, standing at their kitchen sinks washing dishes, could vaguely see their boys in the woods. Even in leafy, summer months, they could hear them yelling and chopping trees. From what they could see and hear, the mothers were reasonably comfortable about this "adventure land." Considering the boys' ages and

14

imaginations, it was about as tame as it could be.

They did not know the Blackhawks had other "lands," such as the swamp at the end of their street. It joined an old road that went into the deep woods for miles. And along the south side of the tobacco fields, they had other forts, raft houses on large ponds, and a sturdy tree house here and there. Parents would sometimes see evidence of the other areas the gang visited, like wash tubs full of honeysuckle trees and mountain laurel they would sell cheap to local housewives for their yards, buckets of large bull frogs to scare their sisters, and rusty iron blades from Colonial farm tools. It all seemed harmless and they had other kids to raise; and real problems on their minds. The brothers all looked so happy, healthy, and proud. It was hard to imagine they had no safety boundaries.

At times, their explorations would lead them into dangerous situations like wandering inside an old electricity generation building on the Scitico, escaping deadly field fires, and path finding during hunting season. If caught at their favorite shenanigans, they would have been in serious trouble for breaking a variety of laws. Fortunately, escaping capture, even detection, was their natural specialty. Protection of the woods from commercial use was their occupation, even if the larger, adult society disagreed, even if they didn't understand what that meant. These conflicts with some of the neighbors and businesses, the cops and the churches, came to be regarded as a sort of "rap sheet" against The Blackhawks, including:

Assault on a Good Humor truck driver with terra cotta flowerpots thrown from the tops of tall trees.

Setting fire to a dried tobacco field, destroying a half acre of wrap quality tobacco.

Vandalizing two house construction projects by defecating in equipment, removing and hiding building materials, and scattering tar and tacks over a finished concrete floor.

Trespassing on a local dairy farm, arousing a bull and setting it loose in the nearby yards.

Engaging in BB gun fights with other neighborhood youths, injuries resulting.

Unlawfully removing and selling the Official State Shrub of Connecticut, Mountain Laurel.

Breaking and entering Electrical Generation Building, No.3 on the premises of the Powder Hollow Gunpowder Company, Hazardville, Ct.

Impersonating a cub scout to sell Christmas wreathes.

Giving a false confession to a Roman Catholic priest.

If they had a publicist, that person might have shined a light on their brave, and voluntary protection of other kids from bullies, including their work stopping a gang of older boys from setting fire to an old barn, breaking up a pack of roaming dogs, fixing other kids bikes, pulling skaters off cracking ice and other junior rescue missions. And they paid a price for helping, like Keith being stung by a hive of bees to save a puppy. Cary sprained a wrist pulling a little kid from the Scitico rapids, and the expected wounds of fighting bullies who liked to gang up on weaker guys. They didn't want a reputation as being "good", or any reputation, as such. They just did what they thought was fair and wanted to be left to doing it.

One thing they were afraid of was boredom. That was why they entertained the notion of meeting their female nemesis in a sexually perilous situation. Those Blackhawks who "didn't want to see any bare girls," were still excited about impressing Rozzy and Jenny with the ingenuity of their fortifications, their powerful effort and ability to transform earth and trees into their creations. It was a new thrill with unknown penalties for getting caught.

Tomorrow came, and the morning routine followed without any parental suspicion. After school at the bus stop, Kevin Somero, biggest of the gang, showed Jack some educationally related material for this secret, show-and-tell. "Just in case we need it," he suggested as he brought out two thin booklets from inside his large ring binder. They were his parents' twin volume Illustrated Atlas of the Human Male and Female Anatomy..

Jack flipped through the thick, colorful pages of the Female volume and commented that after the first couple pages of the naked "Young" and naked "Mature" woman, complete with generative organs, there were only drawings of organs and bones, and a small baby connected to "Pregnant Woman" by some twisted rope.

"If I had a hard-on, I would have lost it looking at all these skeletons," Jack flatly stated.

"Let's take them along just in case the girls want to look at them. You never know," Kevin countered. Who would have guessed this generation would make pornography a billion dollar industry.

Jack agreed. Maybe someone would feel excited to see the books, but not him. He was taking this risk to see

17

the authentic female form, in the flesh, and to compare her body to his, experience the differences in some way he hadn't figured out just yet. Maybe he wanted to touch those differences. What would that be like? What happens after that?

Jack figured Rozzy must want to find something special, something secret about him, as well. Why else would she take this chance? Was it really just to see some logs nailed together into a box? Crawl through some dirty underground paths in exchange for the risk of getting caught with boys in the woods? Or, was she growing curious about the effect revealing her pre-teen body would have on him? Somehow, there was a kick in it for her.

Stopping to throw a stone at a telephone pole, Jack cleared his head of those thoughts to concentrate on the action that was about to begin, his plan that was about to unfold. But instead of mentally rehearsing the steps of the scheme, he felt an unusual emotion interrupt: fear. This fear brought intense energy to his brain, then to his body; and then determination to see the plan through to whatever the end would be—anything but boring. He had seen war movies with scenes of new paratroopers-- scared, getting ready to jump out of the plane for the first time, not knowing if the parachute would open; not knowing if they would land alive; if they'd be captured and killed, or become heroes, or maybe just hang in a tangled parachute for days while vultures waited to claw out their eyeballs. Then an old, fat sergeant would push 'em out the door before they could totally panic. Jack was about to push himself out the door.

The Blackhawks all went to school in the first session, so they were home before lunch. When Jack came in to change, he could tell by his brother's faces they had too much time to think-- and worry. He got ready while

18

he joked with them about the books, changing their mood from "pending doom" to "fun to be had." After a quick "see ya later, Mom," they were out the door, headed for the break in the barbed wire fence that separated their yard from the woods. Soon, they picked up the path that wound lead them to the dirt road they called Wilderness Road. They looked toward the swamp. No Blackhawks there. They turned left on the road and headed for the end near the paved street. After a few minutes, Jack could see the other Blackhawks ahead, already sitting on the familiar, log railing.

"We were supposed to meet at the swamp. What are they doin' up there? Kevin better have a guy watching down the street toward Rozzy's house and one checking up the road to Fishers' street," Jack said to Cary and Keith, "Cuz there's trouble living in both directions."

"We shoulda brought our BB rifle with us, Jack," Cary suggested, too late.

"I have something," Jack assured his brothers, "Not a rifle... the BB pistol I got in payback for the "scab lips" Big Donny gave me with that kick in the face last year. It's tucked in the back of my jeans, loaded and pumped. The rifle is hid in the White Birch fort, in the back tunnel, wrapped in newspaper. You and Keith run for it if we get caught in a BB shoot. Maybe that's what Rozzy is up to-- leading us into an ambush with Fuller. We'll see. Her ass will get the first shot if that's her plan..."

"You looked real neat with those scab lips," said Cary as they hurried along, watching around and behind them, 'No class picture for you, Jack. Your face will wreck the picture. Too scary,' Mrs. Westcott said. I can still see Big Donny at the top of the tree ladder, swinging back his combat boot right into your mouth. You fell pretty far, and real fast--thud! And blood...all over your face,

19

swelling up..."

"Shut your face, funny boy, or I'll puff it up for you," warned Jack, "At least his Mom made him give me something for that kick in the face. She thought it was bag of little pirate men. We used those for target practice." he laughed as they approached the other Blackhawks.

Jack was upset to see they were all facing one direction... at him, with their backs to the street. "Ain't anybody keeping a watch out?" Jack whispered sharply. They all shook their heads "no." Within seconds, the result of that mistake was soon made clear and present.

Now Jack was searching for brothers and answers while stealing up the dirt road. He began to accept the fact that one failure—getting distracted by sex books while waiting for naked girls to sneak over-- was enough to break their defenses and send them into hiding. He wanted to find the other Blackhawks soon, before things got worse. Maybe they were in a tunnel.

What luck! Before reaching the tunnel entrance he spotted his gang gathered around the same dead log near the street. Not too smart. At least they were paying attention to what was around them. Their faces brightened as Jack approached and soon they were speaking all at once...and a bit too loud, Jack warned. He asked where they all disappeared to earlier, and if anyone knew what happened to Rozzy, Jenny, and the crazy woman.

Kevin offered his recollection, which wasn't much. All he knew was that after the crazy woman took off, Rozzy and Jenny ran after her, yelling for her to stop. Kevin confirmed she's was Rozzy's mother. The girls were really upset, scared and crying. Mom just kept going. She stopped yelling, though. He and Keith came out from hiding and talked to the girls. They said Rozzy's mom must have heard them yakking about coming over here and followed them. They didn't know she was following until they heard her running into the woods at us.

"Rozzy asked where you were, Jack," Kevin added, "But we didn't know where you ended up. So, they took off for home, I guess. I wouldn't want to be them when the "strapper" comes home. Sorry about taking off. It was a shock to see it...her. We all had the same idea—get the hell out of there. We couldn't even find each other for, like, ten minutes. We knew you'd get away... or shoot her. We heard about the pistol."

"Well, I shot Fuller. I've had a couple things happen to me that you need to know about. We gotta get our stories together, too, before we go home. But we're in sight from anywhere in these woods right now. We can't talk here. Let's go to the...", Jack stopped talking as his eyes fixed on the figure coming fast from behind the line of Blackhawks, pushing straight through them and right at him.

"What the hell?" he silently swore, "This shit again?" She appeared from the opposite side of nowhere, still screaming about kicking balls and whipping asses.

Jack wanted to yell: "Stop! Just who the hell do you think you are that makes it OK for you to come into our woods to beat us with a leather strap?

But he did not get to say one word. Worse than that, this time, he had no chance to run. He only had time to drop his spear across his body and brace himself against the expected collision. She charged up, but stopped short, and grabbed the spear; pulling it and Jack to her while she quickly brought her knee up hard, into

21

his groin. Jack fell to his knees, curled over, and pitched forward into the dirt.

This was not the erotic encounter of male and female bodies Jack was hoping to experience. But it was a new sensation, vividly connecting the pain sensors in his manhood to the pain receptors in his brain. Physically, it disrupted control of his lower body. The feeling was almost impossible to cope with, unlike a stinging punch to the nose or face, or even to the groin's cousin, the gut, which ached like hell but left him able to fight on. Big Donny's kick to the mouth was not as debilitating. This knee was personal. It twisted and soured the depths of his lower regions to the point of nausea, leaving him momentarily incapacitated, unable to even open his eyes, or talk. He could hear her cursing as she crouched over his body; and feel her fingers trying to loosen his hatchet from the rawhide strap. He managed to grasp the spear lying under his chest.

He could not panic. He didn't feel good enough. Jack thought about some judo moves his father had taught him, but he was already on the ground. So far, he only knew flips and take-downs. So it was his mother's words that guided his actions: "When you're losing the fight, just be sure you hurt the other person." Strengthened by her order to inflict pain, he elbowed Mrs. Corsa in the ribs. This allowed him some room to crawl out from under her, turn as he rose to his knees and ram the spear butt into her exposed belly. His balls felt a little better. The blow left her on the ground, quietly gasping for breath.

Jack was too weak to do more damage, so he hobbled toward the nearest tunnel entrance to disappear for a while. She would finally go home, or go look for her daughter. In the tunnel, Jack could hear only his breath and the rub of his jeans against the tunnel floor. After a

22

short time, he heard leaves swishing, felt a slight pounding on the ground coming vaguely toward the tunnel route. Snap! Snap! Fump! Something hit the tunnel floor. He heard her familiar yell.

Jack hoped she broke her leg so he wouldn't have to shoot at her with his BB gun. He felt for the pistol at the back of his jeans—it was still there. He kept crawling, and then stopped.

"Maybe I should just fire a BB at her as a final warning. Better that than pulling my hatchet out, cuz she's crazy making this for real. If it comes to it, I'm using everything I have and leaving questions for later."

"Jeeesus Chrise!!! You sonofabitch, bastard. Oh! God!!! My fuckin ankles, my ankles ... shit..." she could barely scream. Jack turned around to face the tunnel behind him. He held the flashlight head against his palm so he could slowly allow light into the tunnel. She had fallen through, ripping her top off on a sharp branch before her red Keds came to a sudden, bone twisting stop on hard packed clay. The flashlight revealed her scratched, half-naked body sitting on the tunnel floor. The ponytail stayed flipped toward him, while she looked at one ankle, then the other. Finally, she threw her head backward and sighed, looking at his light. It was odd to see her at rest. Jack began to notice small, black ropes on her legs and white shorts... they were moving...they... were little snakes! And beside her shoulder, its head raised, was the mama snake, its jaw partly open, ready to strike the intruder.

But the mama's jaw could not fully open. Her eyes and brain were fixed on the bright beam from Jack's flashlight. The little snakes kept moving around, though, not looking toward the light. They were busily winding in and out of her short-shorts, their tongues flicking, seeking

23

out the best spot in the warm area at the top of Mrs. Corsa's legs. She didn't notice these slick, persistent explorers right away, due to the numbing pain from her ankles. But now she was seeing the twenty or thirty of them and it was like crabs on ice-water for her. She screamed at them, ripped at them, flung them against the wall, and pounded them into the floor. It was hard to see if they had teeth but they snapped at her hands as though they surely thought so.

Jack couldn't decide whether he wanted to help the she-devil or enjoy the antics of the baby snakes. The little guys were winning. Mrs. Corsa couldn't get them out of her shorts, so she pulled her legs up together and pushed her bottoms down past her knees, the better to sweep the slippery wigglers away. Now Jack could see nearly all those parts and places shown on the "good" pages of Kevin's parents' book. But this was not how he imagined his first sight of the form and movement of a naked female body would make him feel. Not that she wasn't moving up and down, opening and closing a matched pair of toned and tanned legs, breathing hard, screaming a little, and talking dirty [though Jack was not yet aware of any relationship of the latter to sexual intercourse]. Jack had to admit that knowing she was in pain and not feeling pleasure shut off his sexual arousal...just wouldn't work.

It was time to help Mrs. Corsa out of the tunnel. The hard part would be reaching her while keeping the big snake from finishing its move. So Jack crawled toward the two females on his elbows and knees, keeping the light in the snake's eyes with one hand, and his spear in the other hand to poke the snake away or use to help Mrs. Corsa get up and out from the tunnel.

If it weren't for his aching balls being dragged along the ground, he might have had a laugh at how

24

bizarre this intimate encounter with Mrs. Corsa's private parts was unfolding. For the closer he crawled to her, the closer he came to the big snake. He thought it might be worth it if she appealed to him in some way.

"Mrs. Corsa, I'm coming to you with a spear to scare the snakes away. And I have a light that's freezing the big one next to you so she doesn't bite. Ya hear me?" She responded with a hoarse command to get her out, NOW!

Jack kept moving and shining his way to this poor victim. The tunnel was quite deep here and he was able to stoop.

"Help me," she pleaded, "I'll brush off these little pricks and you pull up my shorts."

"I can't pull up your shorts with one hand. I need to keep the light in the snake's eyes. I'll brush with one hand and you pull up your shorts with your two hands." Her look of disgust said she didn't want to do things that way, but she knew she had to go with that approach; and it worked.

"Now, give me the spear", she commanded, "And use your hand to s-l-o-w-l-y push up as I pull myself up on this fuckin' stick. Now! Easy! That's it, easy... now a bigger push. Up! OK, I'm above the hole. Oh, Dear God, I'm up on my elbows. Get up here! Get under my armpits and pull me out, now."

First, Jack had to let the light down from the snake's eyes. Fortunately, with the little ones safely behind her, she shot past him without a bite. They all followed her down the tunnel to a new hideout. Jack hurried out of the tunnel to Mrs. Corsa. Squatting behind her, with his arms locked together under her armpits and

25

gritty bare breasts he was just able to lift her up into a sitting position. She was two swollen ankles ready for rescue. Jack gave her his undershirt to wear. There was no "Thank you." no apology for kneeing him in the balls. Jack began to painfully walk toward home, yelling over his shoulder that help would be coming soon. Despite her pain and his effort to rescue her, she started a word attack.

"You are a stupid little jerk, mister. You had no business tricking my daughter into coming out here with your stupid tunnels, hidden holes ... and snakes."

Jack had enough of this person. She was a bully. "Poor Rozzy," he thought, "No wonder she wants to learn about a place to hide."

"You have hidden holes, too...in your head," Jack shot back, "Makes you as moony as the river down there. That King snake wouldn't hurt anybody. They eat other snakes, but not their own. Unlike you; I know you beat your daughter—Mrs. Child Beater." He was getting into it now that he had totally lost respect for her authority, "And your smokes—they must be real good for your kids to breathe."

"Don't think you can tell me what I can do with my own children. You are a filthy boy who brought my daughter out into dangerous woods to play 'doctor' with her," she answered with all the breath she could gather.

"I trust these woods more than you. They protect all kinds of stuff. But we saw a barrel of gunpowder go off today. It had a ponytail for a wick and somebody lit it with a cigarette." He thought that wisecrack was good enough to shut her up.

Jack turned to continue his bow-legged walking,

thinking these woods would never feel the same again. For one thing, the Blackhawks would be split up for a while. Not for starting this thing-- his parents would listen to all the "facts". They didn't side with grown-ups if they didn't act grown up. But everybody who had something to do with today's skirmish would be in a gold fish bowl after this, including Mrs. Corsa.

"Don't ever come near Rozzy again." She was back to giving orders.

"She'll get a good beatin' for what she's put me through. Causing me to fall into one of your sick tunnels where you could put your dirty hands all over me. Maybe now you think you know something about women. Well, you don't! " Mrs. Corsa spit the words at him.

"I sure hope not. I'm thinking you're one of a kind. For Rozzy's sake, I hope she has a better father, but it's all pot luck. He could be a rat, too; or maybe he's just away too much. But if either one of you hurt Rozzy again, I'll ask my parents to report you to someone who can put you behind bars. Or, I could tell Rozzy and your husband how you got to see the tunnel. I wish I had my Brownie..."

"You listen to me, punk. When I see my husband I'll have him go ..."

"For your own good" Jack shouted above her coming threat, "Don't send anyone to my house with stories. My father is a decorated Sharpshooter and a gentleman, and my mother trained as a school nun. I wouldn't want to be you if I showed her your strap. You know the one. The one you brought to whip her sons' balls. It has your husband's initials on it."

Even Mrs. Corsa knew that hard evidence would be tough to deny. Jack sensed her bravado shrinking,

27

sense her sudden rear of the how other adults would view her actions. Jack was feeling relaxed enough to dish out some threats of his own.

"Rozzy goes to Catholic school. Did you go, too? Ever feel a nun's cold fingers suddenly grip the back of your neck? It chills your whole head, right? Your eyes close, your hair stands up, and you drool a little. My mother never does that, but my aunt, Sister Marguerite, showed us how to use that grip to handle bullies. She and my mom also have these wooden Rosary beads—real strong, not like plastic ones. I've seen them wrap these beads real tight around their hands, like brass knuckles. They don't use them for hitting. They use them to pray for things, like healing. I think your ankles might heal faster if you treated Rozzy better...stop hitting her when you have a problem ... or you could wind up hiding in tunnels and doing a lot of praying."

"Gotta go, I'll send help. You really need it. And I'll need my undershirt back when it's cleaned, please."

MY PAPER ROUTE

I don't want to sound too whiney, but summer can suck— suck a person in to believing everything is going to be fantastic for months, just because the air should be warmer, days longer, school is closed, and people go on vacation for a couple of weeks. Sure, I've had one or two outstanding summers, and some good ones. Even those summers resulted in raising expectations beyond reach for the next summer, leaving disappointment as the strongest emotion about summer that I have. This is especially true for summers in my early teens when I was too young to drive, or work-- in most businesses. Summers were bad when returning to school looked more exciting than spending more time in the summer theater of sexual and economic frustration, watching previews of its next feature: boredom.

Songs that touted how wonderful summer would be, like Connie Francis' "V-A-C-A-TION in the Summer Sun," and Jerry Keller's "Here Comes Summer," really pissed me off. Who was having those kinds of summers? I wasn't. But some of my friends had summer jobs that allowed them to get a taste of summer's promises. As for me, I could do anything I wanted all summer, as long as I took seven younger brothers and sisters with me. I knew that would not be possible, so I agreed to bodyguard and feed my siblings during the day while my parents worked two or three jobs just to meet the weekly expenses of a family of ten. I was the oldest of us eight kids, so what could I say?   ...

"Sorry, I'm busy being a teenager right now. Don't you see these pimples? Can't you tell I'm spending all my spare time masturbating? You don't hear my silent rage, and sense my sexual frustration? Maybe after I grow up, we could talk about your problems."

Or: "No can do, Ma. You had all these kids so now you can watch 'em yourself. Make their meals, do the laundry, and all the cleaning. I'll just sit over here reading, or maybe split for awhile and meet with my friends at the town pool to check out which girls are filling out their bathing suits better this summer. Oh! Don't forget to have dinner ready for Dad when he gets home from his day job; and make the bag lunch for his night job, before you leave for your part-time job at the finger chopping, toy factory. Ask Gramma if you need any help."

I couldn't do that even if they had let me. I knew my role and, frankly, I wanted to help out, make sure everybody had an equal chance to survive. It was easy to see a seventy-five year old grandmother wasn't going to be able to ride herd over seven, bright, crazy monkey-people from fourteen down to five years old. Cute, unique, and mostly well-behaved as we were, my younger brother was a wild card. They call them ADHD now. Then, we just knew his behavior as "friendly-dangerous." Without my Jack Nicholson on the wall to protect the weak and brutally punish the tormentor, his fun antics would reduce the number of living children in the house week-by-week. So, while it was the 60's and an optimistic time for most people around my age, I felt fifteen years old going on fifty.

For actual adults without a tribe of kids, there was the excitement of a young, invigorating President; a new generation going to the moon with the "Honeymooners;" a tide rising and all that kind of optimism was in the air. Television was a magically presented entertainment source that brought adult's idols of stage and screen "right into your living room." But TV production was very much in-process, still finding its primary purpose and audience. Programs, as they were called, were mostly news and soaps and test patterns [TV didn't broadcast--wasn't "ON"-- all day and night]. Most of the shows had adult themes, though not adult meaning "R" rated, "adult" as

31

in depressing stories about the realities of everyday life after you've made all your decisions about what to be, who to marry, where to live and similar millstones around your neck.

We teenagers had different crap to deal with than the characters in these shows about raising children. There was live TV drama; Really Big Shews, especially variety shows, but rarely with The Beatles, and maybe one Elvis per year. There were Westerns galore, but no Pussy Galore, no escapist, action thriller stuff... like Star Trek, I Spy, Wild Wild West, as yet. Our Lone Ranger and Superman years were behind us. Lawrence Welk and his bubble boys dominated the TV musical terrain. We were molting, surly teen horny toads, suffering through long droughts between Bandstand and Dobie Gillis. So, although we looked lazy and uninvolved, maybe dangerous, we were just deeply bored, slightly comatose, and lacking purient entertainment; particularly in rainy, cold New England: home of the Puritan moral code with a Catholic guilt additive.

At our age, there was no source to turn to for the stimulating visual image we needed. Nothing...except the "Grand Compendium of Material Things"—The Sears & Roebuck Catalog. Not to imply that I or my peers had money to buy anything presented between its covers, no. But all five pounds of it came in the mail for free, offering a photographic and highly descriptive presentation of what you could buy IF you had money. The Catalog's pictures displayed a wide variety of goods, from models wearing bras of all sizes, to 12 gauge shotguns with an international range of models. There was every imaginable kind of outdoor gear including tents, and canoes, swimming pools and fishing poles.

Everything shown was so precisely described, measured and weighed that the price seemed scientifically validated. Quality was all attested to by experts, visceral descriptions were given of materials used in the crafting of each item so that I could almost smell the leather of the baseball gloves, hear the new, white baseball hit the pocket of the Yogi Berra catcher's mitt, feel the smooth wood of the 32 oz. Nellie Fox bat in my hand. What to wear? Check the clothing sections for sport jackets and snap jacks, or engineer boots for the Mondo in you.

The pages of this Bible of Retail Goods provided a vivid menu for the imagination engaged in material and carnal desires. Still, the viewer/dreamer paid their dues for looking at what was out there. Once I could explicitly see what I wanted and knew it was available, it was either find a way to get it or live unhappily without it. There was no pseudo-Buddhist option at my age to limit expectations and magically conform what I wanted to what I had. There were too many cool things and fervid longings; too many sex and growth hormones flowing through my hungry body and hedonistic mind to put my cravings on hold. "Hold this!" I raged against the expected pit of summer's broken promises.

There was no doubt that a job search was called for, beginning with the choice of a job. My range of choices was very limited; so narrow it was misleading to say much choice was involved. I was too young for a Working Permit, which granted sixteen year olds the privilege of becoming legally hired. My family didn't own a business, an excellent source for under-the-table earnings, and there was no demand, at that time, for adolescent porn stars.

I looked around at what, if anything, my friends were doing for money. My closest friend, Dan, was a professional altar boy at St. Theresa of the Child Jesus, Roman Catholic Church. This was a neat gig: two morning

Masses, at an ungodly hour, in two languages he did not understand, Monday-Friday. Pay: $10/week. Throw in the bonus High Mass, on late Sunday morning, and add another $3! So what if it was long enough to cause hypoglycemic shock in an adolescent metabolism. That was $13, tax-free. But the best part, the gravy boat, was doing a wedding: $5 [from the priest's envelope] about every 2 weeks. Even a funeral could breed generosity, fetch a fiver, at least $3. Dan the altar boy could rake in from $10-$23 per week, average $16. All this earned before noon, leaving the better part of a day free. At noon in the summer, I was still cleaning up breakfast or starting lunch for my younger, seven brothers and sisters. The rest of the day I would guard the younger ones from the older ones. My pay was room and board and an occasional five dollars for night-time babysitting.

But there was a barrier to gaining entry to this lucrative, religious boy's profession: Altar boys' families are usually prominent in the social and charitable activities at the church. For example, their father collected seat money at Mass, or belonged to the charitable laymen's society. Their moms did cake sales, the Christmas Bazaar, or sang in the choir. My parents were very devout, practicing Catholics. They practiced the Church's rhythm birth control method quite frequently [8 babies in 10 years]. As a result, they had no time for non-sexual Church activities. So, although Dan and his dad spoke up for me, I wouldn't find my name much above the bottom of the hiring list. I was impatient for guys to grow out of eligibility. I tried to get one altar boy to become a Protestant, informing him they had no "Confession" requirement. In the end, he decided to face the weekly embarrassment of talking in whispers about his masturbation habits with the old guy in the small dark room and stay Catholic for the massive audiences, the massive marble altar, and more paying masses.

This was very discouraging, and I must have let my disappointment show because my mother wanted to lend some help, despite knowing full well she could not spare me from my shepherd duties. She chimed in with some very corny and bugged out suggestions, like selling lemonade, washing neighbors' cars and house windows, like I needed more scrub work for pennies. Her best suggestion, which she got from some vegetable stand geezer with hair in his ears was, "Go to the potato farm."

This was actually a suggestion to pedal ten miles to a prison-like farming business two towns [cultures] away, largely inhabited by "in-breeds." There was no guarantee of being chosen by the boss to work twelve straight in the hazy sun, bent over, breathing dry, gritty dirt for 50 cents per hour, IF you picked the minimum number of bushels. If the boss wanted to screw you out of making the six bucks, even 3 frickin' potatoes short of the minimum dropped your pay to three measly bucks. I didn't have to apply there to decide it wasn't for me. Uncertain pay for unavoidable pain. No thanks! The only perk I saw was getting a great tan. On closer inspection, even this was a dud at the beach, as it was obvious you got it by working like an anteater: your face in the dirt and your ass pointed at the blazing sun. Bronze Apollo laughed. Another perk, for overweight guys, was losing weight through dehydration. I was already McSinewy. Next suggestion!

Selling Christmas cards in the heat of July seemed a good idea to Ma, thinking it would make people feel cooler just looking at the snowy scenes made of glitter. But in reality, people were spending on fans...as many as they could find... and Christmas was too far away to tie up one's money.

There were other ideas and other schemes, but they also demanded some major requirement I could not

35

meet. If it wasn't age, or connections, or start up money, it was the larger problem of the nation-wide recession that created an over-supply of eager and able, unemployed people with proven skills and families to support. I was not at the bottom of the employment Totem pole. I wasn't on the Totem pole. That situation would change with time, but I needed something right now! This summer! If angry sulking paid by the hour, I would have had money to burn. But angry sulking is not an advertisement for ability and energy. It only pays in clinical depression trials and, sometimes, in professional acting.

I needed something described in the basic Yin/Yang theory we all learned reading fortune cookies or at karate class: I needed to become a positive-vibe person to attract other positive things, such as love, wisdom and a new baseball glove. When good things and experiences are coming your way with the greatest of ease, you're in the Yang phase. Enjoy it— because the Yin phase is already starting. The purpose of this phase is to balance all that happy, fun, "it's all good" state of being by bringing loss and sad situations into your life until your experiences and soul have equal amounts of fun and suffering, fullness and emptiness...a complete cycle of life, repeated often or maybe, once.

I was sure I was then at the bottom of High-Yin. My attitude had become "Fuck it!" The pendulum had swung full arc in the negative direction of stale baloney sandwiches and warm water. Even so, it was about to reverse direction and cut through the cosmic bullshit toward char-broiled cheeseburgers, sodas, and swordfish. I wasn't hipped to how or exactly when it would happen. I only remember I got bored with being bored. I decided to do something different, even if it didn't put a quarter in my hand.

What I had in my hand was a stone. I was just sitting on our front porch looking across the street and beyond the neighbor's garden, at the baseball field and pond in the distance. Just zoning, mentally idling. At some point, my gaze moved back to focus on the old lady weeding her garden in the hot sun. I had watched her working hundreds of times, wondering why she was doing that to herself...all hunched over from bending, wearing a ton of clothes and a heavy kerchief or two, barely able to walk. I thought this behavior was just plain dumb. Now I became aware of myself sitting there, doing nothing with my capable adolescent body, while she was struggling to stay alive to kill one more weed.

Then our dog entered the garden scene—big old Tub-Tub, who was supposed to be tied up in our backyard for destroying a part of the old lady's garden. I called for him, but the smell of chicken shit trumped his obedience training. That's when I knew that the stone was in my hand for a reason. One more call, but he was on his way. My throw caught him right behind the shoulder. The cramping pain folded his front leg and caused him to slide safely into the grass in front of the chicken yard. I ran over and checked him out—he gave me a big wet tongue slurp across my cheek. I apologized to the old lady, expecting to see anger in her eyes. Instead, she looked sad that I had to wing my dog. Her face was more creased and puffy than my grandmother's mother, but her eyes were still clear blue and alive. She nodded her head when I spoke, like she understood my apology, and then waved for me to follow as she walked over to her side porch and brought out a box of strawberries to give to me. As far as I knew, I had to take them. Then I thanked her, and took Tub-Tub back to jail and some water.

I gave the fruit to my mother, keeping a few for myself. She told me that Old Lady Lachowitz and Mr.

Lachowitz were peasant farmers who came here from Poland after the First World War. They were also the grandparents of the Glenaugh brothers, who lived in the house on the other side of the garden. Their mother was the old lady's daughter.

Imagine that...an actual peasant! I had read about peasants in a number of history books. They were always in the picture of world events since the Dark Ages, getting screwed by the overlords. Kids my age would read so often about the ass-kicking and apparent lack of smarts and courage of "poor peasants" that "peasant" became code for "loser" or, worst, a loser from a long line of losers. If a kid called you a "peasant," it was a wicked bad insult that signaled he was asking for his face to be punched in. Old Lady Lachowitz didn't act like a loser, though. She and her husband carried themselves [even while bent in-half] like people with great pride in doing what they were doing—making things grow, making food. Her husband died during the winter. It was beginning to seep into my mind that all the work was now on her.

"She's way too old to be working on a farm all day, isn't she? She's not in Poland anymore. The Glenaugh's could take better care of her with the old man gone. It's her mother, for Christ's sake!" I ranted, indignant that adults could be so stupid.

"Jack, she is seventy-eight years old, but she's done that kind of work all her life. Probably went to 'church school' only long enough to learn to read her prayers. Even if it hurts her body to work bent over, her spirit needs to do it. It's what keeps her alive," my mother said in her "think about it" tone.

It made me think about my own grandmother, who was almost eighty years old and still riding herd on a bunch of brats and a two year old. She was so natural at it, knowing just where to be and what to do, that she made it look easy. She was educated and graceful, but a hot "shit" when she let her hair down—literally to her waist—take out her false teeth and scare the hell out of us if we entered her room without asking.

I still had one more question about Mrs. Lachowitz.

"Ma, why don't we buy eggs from her anymore? Tub-Tub?"

"That's just part of it, Jack. I never actually bought eggs from her. I tried to buy eggs from her, but she wouldn't take money for the eggs. She insisted I accept them as a kind of donation. She was concerned because we have a big family. It's only polite to accept generosity, but after a few weeks, I had to tell her I couldn't accept them anymore unless I could pay her something. I have nothing to trade with her. You know. So, this left both of us less than happy, especially after Tub-Tub messed up part of her garden and tried to break into the chicken yard."

"Yeah, I should do something to make up for that, Ma. Tomorrow, when I'm done with making breakfast, and things here are all OK, I think I'll go over there and see what kind of help the Old Lady needs. Just don't think I've stopped complaining about wasting my summer working for free."

"I would never think that, Jack. That would not be like you."

The next day, after the breakfast rush, I looked over at the garden expecting to see the old lady. She wasn't there. I was thinking that it might be too hot to work in the sun, even for her. In scarcely a second, her kerchief-covered head appeared over the rim of the slope at the back of her garden. She had an old metal bucket in one hand and a small shovel in the other. I went over to see what she was doing, which was digging up rotting garden junk she had piled back there, shoveling it into the bucket, then carrying it over to the garden where she'd spread it around between the rows. She gestured with her gnarly, large hands that this stuff was saved last year to feed the garden this year. The chicken shit was in there, too; but not a heavy amount.

"That's good," I thought, because I just helped my father fix our old cesspool and had smelled enough crap for a while.

I said I wanted to help her—no charge; just to make up for my dog's damage. She accepted my offer, but not to take over her gig. She needed shingles replaced on the little barn, the fruit trees pruned, a gutter nailed back, some bushes cut—all stuff she couldn't reach. She rattled the jobs off in her broken English like she had a memorized list in her head. She let me help her for a few hours everyday for several weeks. There wasn't much talk between us. Mostly, she would show me what was broken and the tools to fix it; very basic communication.

One day Mrs. Glenaugh came over to say "Hi" to her mother while I was fixing the latch on the fence. I could hear that they were speaking another language; Polish, no doubt. In a short while, Mrs. Glenaugh called me over to them.

"My mother says, 'Thank you for your help. I hope I didn't ask you to do too much. You are a good worker, for a young person.' I want to thank you, also," the daughter added, and then continued, "Now listen, Jack. My mom is going to be alright with the fix-ups for now. Mickey...you know my son, Mick? He's going to need

40

some help. He wants someone to learn his paper route for when we're gone on summer vacation. It's a paying job. He needs someone he can trust to deliver the papers every day to every house on the route. And he needs a person he can trust with his money.   There are other boys who have already asked Mick if they could do the route. Our family agreed to ask you first. Mick can talk to you about it tomorrow if you'll be home. Okay?"

"Sure. I'll be home. Thank you, Mrs. Glenaugh. I'll talk to my mother about it tonight. She needs me at certain times, but, that sounds great. Yeah. And I want to...well, maybe you could tell your mother this for me? I want her to know it was good for me to work with her. She is a very nice old lady and she should just ask me any time she needs help."

"I'll be happy to tell her, Jack. That's very nice of you. But it's OK if I leave out the 'old' word, OK?"

I was so happy I wanted to run home! Would I want to do a paper route? It was too good to be true! An actual, get-paid-for-riding-your-bike-around, girl-impressing, experience-granting paper route could be mine for the summer? Of course I would want to do it. I wanted to talk to Mickey immediately, before he changed his mind. I didn't need to know the details. I trusted my neighbors to be fair, because they were always fair...often generous. This was an opportunity to make money, to be more independent, more adult. It would have to be some mighty, big-assed problem to stop me from saying "yes". The "mighty" part could be my mother's job. She had a day-job at a candy factory with set hours that I had to cover for her at the home front—taking care of seven kids from eleven to two years old.

My mother wasn't due home from work for another hour. I thought about the best way to bring up the paper route; and decided to let her unwind a bit before telling her the news. The secrecy was blown right away by meeting her at the door and opening it for her...not usual. She was tired, but mothers can read their kids' faces without much effort, and she read my face in a second. For the first time in a long time, it had a sort of smile on it. It wasn't speaking in whiny, ear-grating tones of complaint. She had to sit down.

"Never mind about the bakery delivery. What happened today? Didja' find a buck while sweeping under Gramma's bed?"

"No. I found a job doing Mickey Glenaugh's paper route."

"Oh my God! How'd this happen? Did he get hurt? Is he sick?"

"No, Ma. It's none of those things. Except for the old lady and Mr. Lachowitz, they're all going away somewhere for the rest of the summer, so they want me to do Mickey's route until...well, I don't know. That and other things we need to know before we know if I can do it."

I'm sure it will all work out, somehow, Jack. It's too great an opportunity for you to not grab it. We'll put our heads together on it," she said with an airy confidence. It must have made her feel lighter just to have my constant complaints off her back. She was beginning to get excited about the possibilities of my working when the whole clan came in for "After Work Courthouse," a daily ritual of ours that combined saying "Hi, Ma. Glad you're home", with a screaming, crying, emotional rush at Mother to present their injuries, deny the shit they got into and the chores they missed, combined with requests for all sorts of things.

Gramma, oldest sister Suzanne, and I were Ma's eyes and ears—the Prosecutors. We were also her arms and legs; nurses and cooks; ramrods and peacemakers—the Plaintiffs. The rest of the clan was often either a vic or a perp, or both. Ma depended on us to provide some factual back-up for all the claims. What would happen to our "system" if I was gone for hours during the day?

After dinner, my parents escaped long enough to tell me I had their full support for taking on the paper route as long as the route time could be flexible. My future as a youth of wealth and stature would hang on that question. I went upstairs to do some weight lifting. It always helped to blow off some stress. Closer to the truth, I wanted look built, in case I needed to impress someone.

Mickey came to the front door, not knowing the bell didn't work. Doorbells were hi-tech in an 1888 Victorian Gingerbread with eight haunted rooms and a bell on each floor...and one of the first things to go forever fluky. Mick's yells for me finally brought us to together on the front porch.

His bike, with the paper delivery bag wrapped around its handlebars, stood upright and ready on our front lawn. I figured he must be starting his route as soon as we've finished talking. I wondered if he assumed I'd be going with him. Either way, he started early. This was not good, because I wanted to start after my mother came home from her job.

"I have to get a haircut at Roy the Barber before noon, when he starts drinking. So I'll go over the plan pretty quick, then you can ask questions when I finish. Okay, Jack.'

"Sure. Mickey, one thing I need to ask before you

43

start: your mom said you guys picked me for this job. I just want to know "Why me," if you don't mind."

"It's a lot of different reasons, like uh... when you and your brothers saved my ass in that snowball fight last winter, I could tell you guys had some guts, good throwing arms, and could work together. I know you're smart in school, good at math and all that shit, don't get beat up or pick fights. If I hire you, you'll learn the route faster than somebody else. You can teach your brothers, like I taught my brother, so they can fill in if you get sick or something. And, you helped out my Gram without being asked; for no pay; and did a good job. So, I figure you're honest; you won't try to cheat me. Those are pretty good reasons to pick you to take over the route.   You already have responsibilities, so I figure you can handle the responsibilities. Is that kinda what you needed to know?"

"Yea. I just didn't want it to be because I was your neighbor, like a charity thing. Thanks for offering me this chance. I know I can learn the route and I do want the job. I gotta tell you that I still have to be around here for part of the day with my little brothers and sisters. And I have to be sure I'll get paid for this kind of regular, do- it- daily, kind of work."

"You sure will. But let's start at the beginning— what you have to do to get paid at the end. So, listen up, Jack. First thing: you get your papers at Dell's Hardware, as early as 11, 11:30. I start as soon as they get there, even if I have to wait for them, so no one can steal any of my papers. If you're short, you're screwed. You'll have to buy the papers yourself for the regular price at Nelchris Spa or the drugstore. There are three other guys getting their papers at Dell's, so you can't prove who took anything. When they see you're new, they'll try to fuck with you. I'm gonna tell 'em that if they do, the McIleney's will beat the shit outa them. The most

44

important thing you do at Dell's is count the papers slowly and count them twice." Once you've left, it's too late to go back and get more papers. If there's inserts, put 'em inside the paper. Don't ditch them in the woods. Customers know there's a shopping coupon insert in the Wednesday paper. If they don't get it, they go ape-shit."

Mickey went on to show me the customer list—in order of delivery—with the payment history opposite each name. He made a copy for me and added a note on dangers to expect at any house that had them...like drunken fathers, biting dogs, crazy women, bullies, and houses with weird smells, hornet nests, snakes under the porch, and so on.

He told me I would not get paid for the training week; just a free soda every day at Nelchris. After that, I would get paid whatever I collected from each customer, minus the cost of the papers, which I paid for on Friday at Wilde's Diner. Collection days were Friday and Saturday. He added that I couldn't be short on the paper bill--ever. He could lose the route. Any current back-payments a customer gave me went to him. He wanted me to start Monday. The job would be mine until he came back on August 28th. If I did okay, he'd ask me to fill in for him at other times. The experience might make me the #1 guy to get the next route that opened up in town.

"What do you usually make, Mick?"

"If everybody pays, and I average an eight-cent tip, ... about eight bucks. If you can collect a big "overdue" owed to me, like over a month, I'll split that with you. Just don't drop anybody, keep delivering. I'll do the dropping when I get back."

It took Mick almost three hours to do the whole route of fifty-three papers spread over three miles of early suburbia. To finish in that time meant going straight through: no stops, no fuckin' around, and no eating until supper. In the beginning, it would take more time for me to finish due to finding secluded houses, missing a house and having to go back, stuff like that.

I didn't want to tell Mick that the timing couldn't be worse: right in the middle of my mother's shift. I had kept my attention on the route info and the amount of pay. But ever since he said I couldn't begin until 11:30, I felt a sick feeling come over me, like the time I lost change from a $20 walking home from the meat market. I should've known it was too good to be true. The route is right in the middle of my mother's shift.

"You still with me, Jack? You're staring out into space, guy. Can you start learning the route Monday, or what? I need to get to Roy's before he's bombed. Last time I came home with half my head cut. I ain't shit'in ya. Honest ta gawd, I had a crew cut on one side of my head, and my same hair on the other side. My old lady shit a brick, cuz' he still charged the whole amount. She went down to "The 4 K's" and told the owner not to sell Roy a drink before noon and never with a customer in the chair or she'd go down to City Hall about his license. That's the problem with having a barber shop with a connecting window to a bar, ya know? Anyway, whadaya think, Jack?"

He offered his hand, and I shook on it, like a zombie in a trance. Mickey left for, hopefully, a complete haircut. A few minutes later, trying to figure out why I didn't just say 'no', I realized I might have been thinking Dan and Bobby could take it, together. I'd stay home, and maybe get more allowance because they were bringing in money. Yeah, that's what I was thinking. I could give that explanation, straight-faced, to my mother.

46

It was a good thing I had an explanation for my unapproved decision, because, in a surprise move, my mother called home on her lunch break. She wasn't into trying to catch me off-guard. Calls to home were rare. She said she couldn't wait any longer to hear about the talk with Mickey. I gave her the whole story, including my "snap" decision to accept. I heard her sigh loudly when I mentioned the daily start time. I guess my decision didn't surprise her.

"You can be dense sometimes, but it was better than saying you couldn't do it. That would be closing the door right there, without a chance to figure something out. This way...well. We'll see what can be done. I have to get back to work, Jack. You did the right thing. Keep an eye on Dan. Bye."

My mother was usually home by 3:20. It was now after four and still no mother. She doesn't shop until she stops at home. Gramma and I started to think she may have finally decided to run away. No—she soon appeared looking tired but pleased. I assumed this was all about me, and that she must have a plan to work the paper route into our family's routine. I closed the sliding doors between the double parlors so we three could talk privately in one of them. "After Work Courtroom" was postponed until further notice. I brought Ma her coffee and Gramma her tea so they wouldn't get stopped in the kitchen. A glass of beer for me slipped by un-noticed.

"Dennis is going to let me go on second shift: three to eleven. First, I had to see if I could get a ride with Nancy Hanson. She was glad to have someone to ride with at night, so that worked out. Second shift pays twenty cents more an hour, too. Ma, can you take care of things while I get ready and until Jack finishes his route?"

47

"What's she saying?" Gramma looked over to me, "Until you come home with fruit, Jack? What fruit, Betty?" She looked pissed off.

"Not fruit, Gramma, 'route', like paper route." I said with enough volume so that she could hear me. I can make money doing a paper route if you can watch the kids by yourself for about an hour. Ma's gonna be here during the day 'till about 2:30, then she'll get ready for work. Most days, I'll be here before she leaves." Gramma nodded agreeably with that proposal.

I turned directly to my mother and lowered my voice so Gramma couldn't hear me. "I really appreciate this, Ma, but can we safely leave the whole house to Gramma? Some days are pretty bad. A lot can happen, even in an hour. It doesn't take a long time to cut Ellie's hair, light the flat roof on fire, bring home more dogs... "

"Your father will have to have a long talk with the older kids about behaving. You know, sometimes they just act up to get your goat. They may be better with you gone. Really, I think it will be okay. You father could get more done on the dining room at night. Gramma could go to bed earlier. Remember, you'll still have to make lunch, and watch the kids at night. Think you can you do that plus the route?"

"For eight dollars a week, I can do a lot, Ma. It's not altar boy money, but I can sleep later and keep my sins to myself."

Gramma pulled herself up with help from her cane and left the room, saying: "Get one of your chums to help you." Chums? Where do old people get these words, I wondered.

I told my mother some of the details of the route.

48

She listened, sipping her coffee, until I finished the basics. She looked a bit concerned for me. At the same time, she also seemed to be laughing inside at how serious I was becoming about this great responsibility.

"At least you'll be your own boss most of the time; no timecard to punch. Just don't screw up Mickey's route or I'll be hearing about it for years from his mother. Enjoy your weekend, Jack. Monday, you'll finally reach your dream of joining the ranks of the working people."

It had to rain on Monday: a strong, steady rain. We both wore hats, but I was pretty sure Mick got a complete haircut on Saturday. We were forced to go as fast as we could to keep the papers as dry as we could. It was fucked up how customers would expect their paper to be dry when everything else in their outside world was soaking wet. We had no plastic bags then, only damp canvass. The rain made hearing very difficult, too. So Mick didn't get to teach me much, except that you had to deliver the paper in any weather.

On Tuesday, I could sense that Mick felt some pressure for losing one of our training days to rain. He didn't joke around, just called a name from the list and handed me the right paper. The "name" was usually the occupant's name. But Mick didn't feel obligated to update a name on his list if someone new moved into a house. It was still "Johnson", even if they had moved years ago and been replaced by a Gagnon family [according to the mailbox].

Mick would also use a description of the house for a "name" if he didn't know the name or had trouble pronouncing it. So "Gray house, Times and Globe", meant a two- toned grey tenement with a Blackstone Times to the lower apartment and a Boston Globe to the upper floor. If a house got a new color, the "name" didn't

49

change if that resulted in two houses on the route with the same color. There could only be one "white house". If another customer switched house color from brown to white, they'd stay "brown house" on the list, not "Hall Ave. white", or "white II". So I had to remember that the white house I'm looking for on this particular street is the "brown house" on my list. The Mick had his own system.

A danger could also be used as a list "name". There was a customer listed as: "dog house". The problem was that several houses on that street had a dog outside. Almost every house had a dog, and they were all dangerous to some degree. So a "dog house' label meant real trouble for a carrier [our official title with the newspaper distributor]. Mick taught me the defensive precautions to take and how to use them. He carried a pocket of half-dollar size stones that were chosen for grip-ability. Hit a dog once and you would only need to cock your arm to make them back off. He actually liked dogs, and got most of them along the route to like us after a few deliveries. They had a job. He had a job. "Let's work together" was the message he tried to bring. Mickey actually introduced me to them, showing them that I was with his "pack."

Big dogs that were beaten by their owner with a folded newspaper could not be made "friends." Mickey told me to look for that thing the dog was supposed to be tied to before looking for the dog. The dog could be in the house. But if the porch railing was ripped off, there was a loose biter somewhere—check for throwing rocks on the ground. Stones didn't have the stopping power to check these abused animals. Mickey made the point that it was okay to skip the house and call the owner about the dog. Never throw the folded paper into the yard...the dog would be tearing while you're busy buying another paper.

Human dangers were usually hard to describe in one word. However, "drunk" was perfect. No need to be judgmental and add "bum." "Asshole" was short, but too general. Adults were mostly assholes. It was easier to assume, unless Mick noted otherwise, [such as "good tipper,"] that they were all assholes of some stripe. I was proud to see my own house on the list as "Prow-gt [good tipper]. There were more than a dozen names on the list that I recognized, including Dan, my altar boy friend. His house was also a good tipper. With his dough, they could afford it. I would soon learn, however, that most of the people with the best houses and cars didn't tip well, but expected great treatment. Poor people, families with paperboy- aged kids tipped the best. They valued taking care of their own.

Never written down, so mother wouldn't find out, were the girl and women problems on the route. Mickey conveyed the details of these cases only verbally. There were temptations, but Mick advised me they were not worth the trouble that came with the fun. Psychology courses were way down the road for me, so I couldn't tell if this was Mickey talking, his parents talking, or his experience from watching his parents, talking. But I was pretty sure he didn't know from experience what the consequences were. We all knew about condoms, but no one could buy them. There was pregnancy awareness; sex-diseases, gooey and painful, were talked about, at length; and, if caught, we expected the girl's boyfriend, brothers, and father would have the right to beat and, maybe, kill us.

"Besides" Mickey added, "If you were screwing someone, you'd fall behind on finishing your route and probably lose some tips."

Bet your ass. The carrier worked to earn money, not to drop his bag for every early bloomer and bored bosom on the route that looked do-able. But it was something to make the route interesting--like avoiding robbery and beatings from older punks. That would also add time to finishing the route without giving anything in return. Knowing this, Mick used his peer friendships to establish ties to their older brothers who became protective of Mickey in the same way that they protected their younger brothers. This protection meant only they could torment and shoulder punch you or extort from you. No one else allowed -- you were a "protected" guy. On Wednesday, I got to see how this system worked.

It started when Billy LaMontagne, another carrier from Dell's, who was almost sixteen and way bigger than us, grabbed Mickey's bag for two papers Billy forgot to order for his new customers. Mick tried to get them back, but a good shove from Billy told us we could not take the guy. Mickey could have taken the papers from the next guy's share, but Mick wasn't like that. He got robbed; he would settle it with the robber. At his order, I started the route by myself while he went right to the McIleney's house. They were three crazy tough brothers, all muscle and slicked black hair, with fast cars and built girlfriends. They hung around with the Wilde brothers, whose mother officially owned Mickey's route, the diner, and the lemonade stand. I started to see this paper delivery business was structured like 15th Century feudalism: Mick was the peasant-serf; the McIleney's were the black knights, and the Wildes were the nobles.

The "Mac's," as they were known, were at the beginning of the route, so I got there while Mick was still around to introduce me. Since they already had a guy lined up for a beating, they were friendly to me...even offered me a beer, just to see if I'd take it. I offered them their paper. Barry grabbed it and stripped it of the Sports section.

"Ma! The new paperboy's here with Mickey! He says you owe him three weeks!" Barry Mac yelled over his shoulder toward the bedrooms.

Mrs. Mac walked into the dining room, looking for a new face. She was an Amazon, in the best sense of the word. Tall, athletic looking, with broad shoulders and a muscled neck. She had a scary, good-looking face and a no-nonsense attitude.

"I don't owe you Glenaugh, unless one of these bums took your envelope!"

"No. You don't owe me a thing Mrs. Mac. Barry's trying to start something. This is Jack Prowse. Just moved to Gardiner Ave. last year. He's gonna take my route while I'm gone with Pat and my folks to Nova Scotia. I'm showing him the route this week and, today, some kid from the other side of the church took two papers from me right at..."

"Some kid? He's bigger than you, I'd bet?"

"Well, yeah, or I'd still have the papers."

She eyed her brood like she was choosing the right weapon for battle.

"Bruce, you go find Mickey's papers for him. And you tell this other kid that he took your mother's paper and to never do that again. And Bruce... tomorrow, I want you to meet Mickey at Dell's. Keep the other paperboys around for a minute. Make sure they all know this new kid is your mother's paperboy. Now get goin'. Mick needs the papers before his route ends."

I was wicked glad she wasn't on Mickey's "flirting females" list.

Before the end of the route, we still had to buy two papers. The ones Bruce brought us were a little shredded, sandy, and bloody. I wasn't the only new carrier the next day. There was someone filling in for LaMontaigne.

We counted out our Thursday papers, and then Mick and I crossed the intersection to The Nelchris for our pre-work soda. We made our choices from the selection in an old, red &white ice cooler that was long enough to lie down in and deep enough for two layers of bottles. It easily fit six bottles from side to side, with the five-cent bottles closest, the ten cent bottles along the back, and the whole smorgasbord of colors and flavors surrounded by mirror-clear, solid cubes of ice. We could have stood there all day trying to decide what to buy, but whatever we picked would be a winner. I decided on Birch beer, cuz you couldn't get that flavor in a supermarket. Mick grabbed his usual: a Smitty's draught root beer. As agreed, he bought the sodas. I had some money that day, so I bought a small Table Talk blueberry pie for myself, while Mickey chose ten cents worth of penny candy, each piece hand grabbed and bagged by Old Hannah. He preferred the candy to a pie because, "You could eat the candy over a longer period of time." He made it last the whole route.

Today, the whole route would take a long time because it was "test day". I would make every delivery under Mickey's watchful eye. Almost half of the customers lived along one, long avenue that gradually climbed to the top of a hill, then crossed a busy, four lane street that gradually rolled down toward the road that circled the neighborhood pond and ball field, where the next largest number of customers were grouped. Unfortunately, a large number of customers' houses were out-of-the way places that took as much time to deliver as a dozen houses somewhere near each other. In today's business world, they'd have to pay a surcharge for playing "informed hermit" on our dime.

The first delivery was the Bourget house, then Biziak's, Draper's and the Drew's. Next was the McIleney's, throwing the route out of a neat, nearly alphabetical start. If paper carrier's ruled the world, everyone would live in alphabetical order. What was this shit, anyway? People living wherever they wanted just because they liked the house or could afford it; living up and down the hills, off into the woods on a dirt road with a gang of mad dogs and muddy, little kids; or in a foundation with no house on top, just a tin and tar roof with some white stones sprinkled on it. On TV, I had seen houses with trees growing through them, and houses with a trout stream dividing the knotty pine, living room. These people were misguided rich artists without kids. They were so far out in the wilderness they didn't need a paper, just a short wave radio. Our special customers were not that type...just way out.

Like Mick, I had to learn to take the dangerous deliveries with the easy double deckers; the hot sun and drenching rain with the ice cold soda and moist blueberry pie. It was all about taking the good with the bad.

We continued along with me in the lead as I casually introduced myself as: "Jack, filling in for Mickey," at each new meeting with a customer. With only three delivery days left before actually taking over, this simple phrase grew in importance for me. Being in-charge of certain duties in my own house was part of being the oldest brother in a large family. And I did it well. But if I made a mistake, there was explanation and forgiveness. This would be my first job in the outside world, where people were not as inclined to understand a mistake, but quick to find one, even invent one if they felt like it. I

55

looked at Mickey. He was confident in how he got the job done. I was aiming to see him have that same confidence in me.

Soon, we were half -way through the route and I had made only one mistake.

"Shit! I forgot to bring Coach Horricks some new baseballs for the game at four o'clock", Mickey remembered, "Keep going, Jack. I'll catch up with you later."

This emergency turned out to be a little trick the Mickster used to covertly observe a trainee working alone. It didn't take too long for me to figure out he was checking deliveries behind me. Dogs were barking again on the route ten minutes behind me. And the barking trailed on at the same pace I was moving. What the hell, Mick had to know if he was leaving his source of dough to some slouch. When he finally met up with me, he looked pretty mellow for a guy out of candy; so I figured he found no mistakes. Tomorrow would be collection day #1, Friday; and payday for Mickey.

I woke up happier on Fridays, and I didn't need a pay envelope coming to feel that way. In America, we are literally programmed to love Friday. So many grinds end for the better, and a number of good things are scheduled to start happening. It's the end of the school week for kids; the end of the work week for most adults; dance nights all over town; fish &chips dinners, especially for Catholics; and by Friday, many people have money in their pockets again, even if only for a short visit. Mick looked like Friday was his favorite day, too, when he came over smiling; carrying a skuzzy, cloth pouch tied to his belt. I couldn't help but stare at it, wondering what it could be used for except maybe carrying live worms in dirt. Mickey patted it with glee in his eyes.

"Got anything to carry money in, Jack? Bills and change?"

"I have an empty wallet. Is that any good?"

"Not really. Where you gonna keep all the change you're gonna collect? And next Friday, when it's your route, you'll need to fit a pad, pencil, and pay list in something bigger than a wallet. See what you can get. Hurry up."

I went back into the house and looked around. My father had tool boxes—way too huge.

"Ma!" I yelled, "Got anything I can use to carry change in that isn't a pocketbook? I need to carry money I collect on the paper route, most of it change."

I have to say, my mother had a way of knowing what I would need before I did. And, one of her brothers was a paperboy. She put a real change maker on the kitchen table. Only the ice cream man had a change maker like this one.

"How about this?" she asked in a droll tone.

I belted it to my hip and started pushing the rings. It wasn't new. It was better than new because it looked broken in and, therefore, I would look like I had experience in using it.

"It's real neat, Ma. How'd you get it? It's not a toy thing, it's made to last. I'll pay you for..."

"You'll have to pay your Uncle Johnny for it, if we see him again. Don't put any bills in the clip. Somebody will grab 'em. Keep bills in your sock, with an elastic...here...around the top of the sock. Don't forget to be back to make swordfish tonight. It was on sale."

I thanked her again [no hugs-- she was English] and I went out to join Mick, who laughed at the changer, shaking his head.

"How can you laugh at this with that shit bag on your belt?' I asked him.

We counted and carried, pedaled and walked, knocked and yelled, collected and billed, all while carrying a small smile in our gut somewhere that grew with the weight of our money holders. Then we saw Mickey's brother screwing up Pine Street on his bike, trying to catch up to us.

"Where's the fire, Pat?" Mickey yelled to his brother as soon as he saw him. Pat just kept his head down, pedaling like a bastard.

"Mickey! It's Bobcia!" Paddy tried to yell when he got near us. We rode down to meet him. "Bobcia just died, Mickey! She's dead. Mom needs you back home-- right now. Dad's at work and she's all shaking..."

Mickey tried to calm his brother down. "OK, Pat, we're coming." Then he began slowly walking around in a circle, looking down, stopping now and then to glance at me.

"Can you finish collecting, Jack?" Mick looked at me with a face as saggy and gray as his decrepit pouch.

"Sure I can, Mick. But what's wrong? Who's Bobcia?"

"My Granny just died, Jack."

I finished the Friday Collection for the first and last time. Mick gave me all he made that week, and I continued to deliver while he had wakes and a funeral to attend [Dan, the altar boy, made a fiver]. Mrs. Glenaugh decided to bring her mother's garden to harvest one last season, so the Nova Scotia trip was cancelled, and Mick's need for my services disappeared with the mourners. I thought I would feel more than my usual, superficial sense of sorrow for some other family's loss of a relative. After all, I saw how hard she worked for years, and actually worked with her for weeks. She was generous and kind—deserving of some tears. Instead, I found that my loss of hope for a summer job was all I could feel. In a few years, I would have used "ripped off" to describe my situation. "Gypped" was the current word for how I felt about my treatment by the One who rewards the sowing with reaping. The Old Lady got gypped, too.

Anger was my dominant emotion: even while laughing, or feeling horny, I was angry. It was not the vague, sulky, anger-lite of early summer, when my mother was grooming me for a potato picker. This anger was born in the gut, not the mind. My expectation of having disposable income had been totally elevated, and not simply because I had invested time and labor into becoming a paperboy. I even brought my mother's job into the effort, and I liked the job. I met my customers; and touched the money. I had a job with a start date. Then it was gone--nobody's fault, just didn't happen. But I felt cheated after trying, and that a vague promise had been broken.

I was aware I was not one of those starving, poor Indian kids my father kept photos of in his "secret" jewelry box. I was a healthy, white, middle class, spoiled complainer with a great future in anything requiring

59

higher learning. My parents loved me, gave me the freedom to explore life, question dogmas, and taught me whenever I'd listen. I lacked very little from my family. But what little I lacked dropped my sense of inner satisfaction quite out of proportion to my actual circumstances. I felt I was owed a replacement job; and someone had better do something about it before, like one of the mad dogs on the route, my collar broke and I did something irrelevant.

What would be irrelevant? Maybe smashing through a cracked window in my school so a gang of us guys and a few daring girls could play on the gym basketball court, talking fast and loose about shirts vs. skins and team showers. Not only did we do that, but we escaped unseen, only to be ratted out by the guys we didn't let into the gym. We didn't let them in because we knew they would wreck stuff just for the hell of it. This was the immediate payback.

The police brought me right to my front door. They insisted on knocking, then telling my parents why they escorted me home. My parents couldn't find any relevance between what they claimed I had done and my normal behavior, ambitions, or hobbies. On second thought, they often wondered aloud whether I ought to become a lawyer, and not a priest. This incident would introduce me to the world of the lawyer, the police, the courts, and the magic these agencies of justice could perform. So there was wiggle room for relevance, after all. My co-defendants and I were immediately on the hook, wiggling. The district court wanted to know the relevance of our acts, which grew by the minute on their tally sheet: Why did we do it? Never once were we asked if we did it, just why. They had to know.

They had to know why we knocked out ten expensive windows, threw dozens of boxes of food on the cafeteria floor to rot, destroyed twenty-odd typewriters, and split several, large slate steps. My co-defendants I and were also becoming curious about these numbers and the wide swath of our wrath. We told the cops we liked the caf food; none of us took typing; and these nine other windows and steps had been broken before we started attending the school. We expected that topless basketball would be our crime, but they never bothered to mention that, nor did we...to protect the innocent.

My mother thought the questions of "who" and "why" and "how many" would all be addressed at a hearing or trial of some kind, like on "Perry Mason." She was mistaken. We were all youths, under the protection of the Juvenile Court, which meant our names had to be kept out of the papers. So we didn't get a trial; an opportunity to confront our accuser, and deny allegations because that would have resulted in publicity which would break the primary rule: keep names of juveniles out of the paper. Our rights were sacrificed to that rule. So we were considered automatically guilty, no trial needed and no names printed in the papers. I wondered what happened to the idea of automatically considered innocent.

No trial, but there was a sentencing. The court didn't leave that out. Our parents brought us to a hearing room in the Civil War era courthouse the next morning. It stunk. Not just the rip-off, but the building. It smelled of a hundred years of trapped air and steam heat spent trying to maintain warmth during New England winters. We did get to meet with a judge, who arrived at 8:00 a.m. already holding an accounting of the exact total of the cost of all vandalism suffered by the school since it opened. Ma suspected the court was only interested in setting the exact number of vandals to divide into the total damage to settle all matters. Now, she was not mistaken. We were going to be the fall guys for all previous, unsolved acts of vandalism. So the number would be 5. Five was the number.

His Honor was not content to read the bill for damages, and proclaim us "...ungrateful cowards, lucky to be spared the "Boy's School." He also entertained the court with a crystal ball reading that predicted three of us would return to face criminal charges many times in the future. This sparked a seizure in one of the fathers, an alcoholic who unwisely sobered up for the meeting, not expecting to hear his son was destined to be a Criminal for Life. "You boys could end up like that," the judge warned us, as two cops dragged the poor guy out to his car. We would be mercifully placed on probation for one year, provided we paid restitution for the damages by that time and stayed out of trouble. He did the math: $287.57 each, some amount to be paid each week when we met with our Probation Officer, who would also provide help in bringing us onto the right side of the law.

As we walked out, I noticed our parents looked more shocked than us delinquents at how easily the police court railroaded us into an unfair settlement. They didn't even invite the lawyers. As a possible, future lawyer, I was also pissed for them. My irrelevant actions opened my eyes to how irrelevant justice was to the legal system. The liar who fingered us also needed some justice. For now, we were under their microscope, so we would have to delay physical payback on Al, the fink. Besides, I had to find a job to pay the crooks back, or learn more about the penal system.

Despite the effort and sacrifice to keep our names "secret," word got out. Some of the neighbors called the next day, offering mock sympathy to my parents, who knew they just wanted my parents to know that they knew. The Glenaughs, true to form, didn't say a thing, but sent over a large, fruit basket and a card expressing support. The corner grocer already knew about it, which meant the story was now on the AP wire of local gossip. All my brothers' and sisters' friends, and, soon enough, distant relatives heard of what the priest-to-be had done. I really didn't care. One of our parish priests-- the younger, tough guy priest and not the older, kinder, gentler priest, sped to our house to offer me confession [no, thanks] and to comfort my angry parents. He didn't pick up that my parents were as angry with the judge as they were with me, which is why Father thought he had to take my Earth father aside to caution him against beating me too severely for my sins. "I wasn't thinking of beating him at all, until you mentioned it" was all my dad replied.

He did punish me, however, with orders to dig a new cesspool—in the front yard. This was genius. To begin with, he needed another cesspool for the second washer and out front was the only place on his property that wouldn't violate the city water code. Additionally, by putting me to work in the eyes of the world, he showed that he was making me atone for my irrelevant acts. We both looked good: he was on top of things with the "chain gang" style, behavior mod, while I got a nice tan, some muscle tone, and even a little sympathy. Honest to God! Even if you were a budding criminal, shoveling out a wide, deep hole from hard packed earth and rock under a summer sun will bring sympathy with your blisters. Not only that, but when I could leave the yard and ramble about, I found that my co-vandals and I had become sort of famous, or infamous. Either way, we were news, and kids our age thought that made us cool to know and hang out with ...and slightly sexy.

On the not-so-sexy side of the bad boy image was the fact that there was now a knock against us, a scarlet "V" on our chests, that I felt certain was going to make finding a job impossible in our little town. I was now suspect to any businessman looking for help, something I didn't have to overcome in my earlier job searches. I instinctively adopted a "don't ask, don't tell" strategy and left my probationary status out of the application process. Only problem was that, sometimes, they asked "Were you ever..."

The gang made its first trip to the Probation Office in one car. It was the first time in a few weeks that we had been allowed to see or speak to each other, so it was a loud ride. Poor Mrs. Brullet drew the wrong month to be chauffer. Through all the glad talk, the sad talk, and the mad talk, I picked up that they all had money to lay on the PO. I didn't. I was not going to take money from my parents. They had enough money problems. I needed to earn some money—pay my own dues, not drag my parents into my trouble. When the summer began, I needed money for attractive, material things to kill boredom. Now, it was needed for keeping my freedom. I sure wasn't going to spend the summer behind a guarded fence with horny, young criminals like myself.

So after we listened to a monotone "do's and don'ts" from the PO, I asked to speak with her after our session ended. The other guys lined up to pay up and grimly walked away with a receipt. While they waited outside in the car, I threw myself on the mercy of this plain looking, middle-aged woman who bore no resemblance to my TV-derived image of the probation officer as a manly, rogue cop who roamed the shadows searching out dangerous ex-cons to push against back alley walls. Still, she had a Canadian Mounty attitude about her. I wouldn't want her tracking me down.

"I'm sorry I couldn't make a payment today," I started my plea,   "But I..."

"You don't have a job. Have you looked for

work?" she asked.

"Yes, I have. In fact I had a job lined up before school even let out. But it fell through because, ah...it's a long story. Not being able to get a job is how I got here; why I did what I did. Doing all the right things didn't work, so I let myself loose. I had to find something that would satisfy me. I did, and now that will cost me. Just want you to know I'm still looking and..."

"I'll stamp your card as 'Attending-no payment,' she declared, pounding my card and stopping my plea before I hit full stride. "You are allowed two missed payments before you are returned to face the judge. Good luck."

I wished she hadn't said that. I'd never had good luck, except to be born into a good family. I never won at a game of chance. I was never in the right place at the right time; found anything valuable; called safe when I was out. Frankie figured out why I had stayed to talk to the PO, and offered to buy lunch on his guest check at the place where he worked, the locally famous Jolly Roger's Pizza House, if I would go into work with him. JR's was the coolest place to be and be seen, so I quickly caved and we jumped out of Mrs. Brullet's red and white DeSoto at Jolly Roger's in Northton. Frankie also noted I might get to meet the famous JR himself; the King of Route 21 food and fun. As we walked across the huge parking lot, however, Frankie decided a warning was in order should we actually bump into the owner.

"Roger's not so jolly, Jack. He's a short guy with a short fuse. Looks like a bulldog. He fires at least one guy every Monday night when he comes back to work after his Rotary Club meeting. Sometimes it's a kid in the pizza house or the snack bar, sometimes a mechanic in the amusement park. He throws knives at any guy he sees smoking on the job. His wife, Helen, keeps the books, and Roger, in line. She's always crowing about how Roger donates to orphans and pays more than the minimum wage, but he's a fuckin' nut; storming around all the time like a heart attack in motion.

He wears a gun at all times—even when he's around a hundred kids in Funland. Last year he shot a guy who tried to rob him in the men's room at the snack bar. He's a flipped out camel jockey, man...so just stay awake if he comes up to us. He always wears dress pants and shirts, like he had meetings going on someplace. The truth is that he and his white Caddy never leave this place except for Monday's Rotary meetings."

We were wolfing down a large cheese pie at one of the picnic tables in the grove by the Snack Bar when the sound of rocks being kicked caused us to raise our heads and see the Jolly Rog chugging toward us on his short thick legs, clumsy but determined, like a bull walrus about to establish his territory. We were on the far edge of his colony of tables. The bellowing began forty feet from us, as he was having trouble getting around the wooden cows and right up to our faces.

"Tom! What are ya doin' back here? Punch in! And why ain't ya eatin' the blue plate special? Wastin' your money on pizza?"Jolly yelled at Frankie.

"I don't start for another hour, JR; and the blue plate sucks on Saturday. But the pizza's the best, as always."

"Jerry!" he yelled at me, "Punch in. Grab an apron, a hat, and go to the pizza house."

"I don't work for you, sir. I'm with Frankie for lunch and my name's ..."

66

"See Helen in the snack bar, Jerry, and get the hell to work before I fire the both of you. Now! Goddamit, now! I'm paying you guys to work, not eat. You can't even remember you work here for Chrissakes! Get moving or I'll have the Greek Bull out here to kick your asses into the mini golf course!"

Even Frankie didn't know who or what the Greek Bull was, but we didn't want to find out. So we started for the snack bar, carrying and eating our last slices as we went. I looked to Frankie for a sign that I should actually go in and look for Helen. Frank walked straight ahead like he was not allowed to look at me. I was afraid to look at me. I didn't have a permit to work, no picture I.D., and I wasn't Jerry. But Jolly was following right in back of us. I was thinking he might shoot me if I split off, like a deserter from the Foreign Legion.

"Go ahead in" Frank finally assured me, "She's on the right after the freezer. There's no Jerry, just like I'm not Tom. JR's brain is scrambled. He sees us together, flashes to the cartoon characters, who are always together. So if I'm Tom, you are Jerry. It makes sense...to Jolly."

Frankie found his timecard and punched in, just as JR hip-checked me into Helen's office on his rush to check the fryolators. Roger was not jolly; and Helen was not from Troy. But she was slim, well dressed, and prim; kinda snobby, like a nun with money.

"Fill this out, please. Here's a pen, and I want it back." she said.

It was a very brief application, asking only the essentials. Unlike many of the apps I had filled out, there was no hobby question, no career goal asked for, no references to provide. I suspected they didn't want to

67

waste any time or paper on a rejection and it was easier to throw knives at kids you didn't know much about.

She asked me for my Social Security card and working permit. Not having the permit spooked me and I flipped the scant contents of my wallet on her desk blotter. She picked up my brand new Social Security card, compared its numbers to my app, and then dropped it back in the little pile, picking up another document.

"This isn't a Working Permit. It's a Probation Registration Card. You have left your city without a parent? Are you a runaway from the Boy's School, Jack?" she demanded.

"No, Mrs....."

"Hallalal,.." She finished, knowing I might have said "Jolly." Then I remembered Frankie saying something about "...working in hell for Mrs. Hell."

"Mrs. Hallalal, I continued, I'm only on probation and I need a job to pay back... pay restitution for some things that got broken, but were mostly broken by other guys..."

"What did you do?"

"I took a shower with another guy's girlfriend after a bunch of us broke in to the school gym to play basketball."

"So you broke more than things; and learned there's no such thing as free fun."

"I guess so Mrs. Hallalal. You charge for it here, right?"

68

She looked at me like I was something on the sale rack she liked, but didn't need.

"I don't see a working permit here" she said while flipping through the pile with her pen, "Do you have one, Jack?"

"Not yet. I'm fourteen and a half. Some types of work don't require a permit, right? Are you hiring for a job like that?" She pushed my collection of wallet paper towards me. As I forced it back into my wallet, I felt a large presence behind me that shadowed Helen and most of the wall behind her.

"I want you to go with Jim, here, to the pizza house while I make a few phone calls."

I had some questions about the need for all this fuss, but a hairy, firm hand on my shoulder answered everything I needed to know. This was unexpected, meeting Jolly Roger, Helen of Hell, and the Greek Bull all on one day. Oh yeah—and the courthouse Mounty. I was becoming more concerned about where this situation was headed because there was still time to meet more people in power and authority. I had to be calm, shake it off, the pendulum was about to swing my way.

The hand swung me around toward the exit door. We started walking toward the Pizza House. I noticed his military stride and posture, black hair slicked back, but very short on the sides. He wore the usual pizza baker's whites, with glossy black shoes. Soon, we were inside the back kitchen, which had a room for the staff to change out of their streets and don the RJuniform. He stopped in this area, putting one leg up on a dressing bench, featuring his black socks, and lit up a Camel. Then he began talking and walking around the dough-mixing room, telling me about serving in Africa during the War, tsetse flies and the sleeping sickness, the women in town.

"I've had more ass than a toilet seat" he declared and then jumped from that subject to the dangers of guys twisting another guy's tit for torture kicks: "Never let a guy pull your teat: "Knee him, thorn him, kick him, stab him. It doesn't matter because that teat pinching can easily cause cancer in men."

"We call 'em PT fights" I answered, "I like to end them right away with a punch in the gut." I said. Jim smiled. I figured he would like that direct approach.

"You how to get people to knock off their high beams when blinking yours at them fails? You cross the doubles and drive right at them until they kick them down...don't chicken out."

"You're absolutely right, Jim. I'll remember that when I get my driver's license."

At that comment, he stood and turned to look me over. "Where are your socks?" He spoke very slowly, like he was enjoying this oral part of what I was hoping was a job interview.

"I don't wear any. Nobody my age does. It's cool, and feels cooler, too."

"It causes stink. This is a food preparation area. Should it stink in a room where food is made, Jack?" I could see the "Bull" might turn on me.

"No. But my feet don't stink. I wash, I use talcum powder. It's no big deal."

"Only fags don't wear socks," His large square face

70

was right up to mine, his breath smelled like garlic. "Are you a fag, Jack?" The last guy who came into work without socks was planted upside down in the ice chest over there. That made it easier to put socks on his feet. He found out what cool is all about, wouldn't you say, Jack?"

"He wasn't cool. He belonged there, sure. He definitely did. Disobeyed the rules. You did the right thing."

"Who said I put his head in the ice chest? It happened. That's all."

The phone rang. It was Helen. I hoped she was checking on how well I was picking up the pizza game or, at least, the mine field of Jim's mind.

"Mrs. Hallalal is coming to pick you up. Look outside; she'll be driving her new, white Riviera. Gonna give you a ride somewhere, son. Here's a couple of bucks. Be wearing socks when I see you again."

I could taste the spicy fumes of undigested pizza rising up my throat. This ride wasn't settling well with my sense of relevance anymore than Jim's theory of socks as an indicator of homosexuality. I couldn't think of anyone who gets hired in a car, except hookers. Still, when she pulled up, I got in, despite the leopard skin upholstery.

"I made some calls while you were with Jim. You may have heard that Roger-- his real name is Wayne-- donates substantial money to a number of charities, like the Boy's Club, the local churches, veteran's homes and so forth. Sometimes we have our generosity returned when we need something. I called someone I thought could speed up your work permit. There are times, though, when people can't do us a particular favor. Getting your

71

working permit a few months early is one of those times. We wanted to hire you so you could pay off your damages. I'm sorry we can't hire you at this time, Jack."

"I really appreciate your taking the trouble to pull some strings, but, why make those calls for me? I noticed you had a pile of applications on your desk."

"Wayne--his real name is Khalil-- thought you would be a good worker. He saw you help Frank empty trash barrels one Sunday, just being a friend. He likes people who help their friends."

"Actually, what happened was this kid wanted to beat up Frank, and finally found out where he worked. We heard when he planned to go to Jolly's and pound Frankie out, so we made our own plan. I wasn't there to empty rubbish, I was there punch someone's face. Just to pass the time, I emptied the barrels while waiting for this guy. No big thing. If you don't mind, Helen, where are we going?"

"You sound like you would get along with Jimmy Vanichas—the big guy in the pizza house. I want to show you a paper delivery route in my neighborhood that might be open soon. Would you be interested?"

"Sure, but it would have to be soon-- like in a week or two. When do you think you'll hear about it?"

"I won't hear about it... I'll know about it as soon as we get to my house and I see a newspaper in my paper box-- or I don't." She was moving the Riviera around the narrow back roads of Lincolnshire without banging the humongous field stone walls that guarded each side of the former cow paths.

"The carrier loses the whole route by missing your

house? You do have some pull."

"Not just my house, they've missed the whole route often enough to be warned not to miss work again, or I'd replace them. I'm the treasurer of the neighborhood association, so I can do that. You would think that delivering sixty papers to beautiful houses, all in rows along six landscaped boulevards, for $15 a week would be worth a couple of hours a day."

I wanted to ask about the alphabetical order, but realized she wouldn't dig it. I imagined what a piece of cake this route would be, having every house for six streets. A Neanderthal could do it, and the pay was double what Mickey's route paid on its best week. Still, I felt obliged to ask some questions.

"Any watchdogs?" I asked.

"We have a security service for protection. The pet dogs here are all trained and fit on your lap."

"Drunks?"

"Mostly away at the country club bar."

"Welchers, weirdoes, women..."

"Women who might throw themselves at you, Jack? Our lonely ladies have richer, older boyfriends. I'm afraid a paperboy wouldn't be much to crow about. Secondly, we don't accept weirdoes into our Association. Period. As far as payment for services is concerned, the paperboys receive a check directly from the Association... a generous, tip is included. We deduct $1 for every house that's reported 'missed'. Any other questions, Jack?"

I had one, like: "How do you miss a house when

they're all lined up, one after another until your delivery bag is empty? However, I didn't want to appear sarcastic, so I went with a more business-like question:

"What's the dress code?"

"Wear a shirt. Stay out of the pools, even if invited. Always be polite. You can remember that."

Without slowing down, Helen turned sharply onto a long cul-de-sac of rich –bastard houses, and made a squealing U-turn up to her curbside paper box. She powered down the window on my side for me to check the orange box. I wasn't expecting to be the first person on the block to know my fate, but there it lay, neatly folded in a plastic bag: the Saturday paper for July 13, 1963. I instantly envisioned the July 20th paper's "Court Report" noting that an un-named youth offender was remanded to the Boy's School for one year or until his restitution was paid-in-full. I gave the paper to Helen. She drove me home.

Those who saw me delivered to my house were quite impressed with my cherry ride. Some of the neighbors' faces looked like they wished they had cut their lawn, painted their porch and, maybe, washed the street. My mother did not feel humbled by, or proud of the means of my arrival. This rich woman couldn't give her son a job he needed to stay out of summer detention and Ma was simply angry that a person with so much wealth and pride in her charities didn't just hand me the $287.57.

I never gave that possibility a second's thought. Collecting for Mickey taught me that most rich people don't see any sense in flat-out giving because only the servant sees the extra dime in the envelope. The act of donating has to be part of a system that shines a light on

74

their goodness and the worthiness of the person who gets the gift.

"Giving me the restitution money would look like she was supporting juvenile delinquency and vandalism," I tried to explain to my Socialist mother.

"Not if she just slipped you cash, ya dope, she chided. She was right. If Helen was poor, she might have given me the money without fanfare; but a poor Helen wouldn't have it to give. Ma was starting to show extra signs of stress over my predicament and her inability to do something to change it.

"The only person who has the money you need is your Memere [my father's widowed mother] and she's the main person we don't want to know about your little crime spree. She still believes you're gonna be a priest. Your father and I have been going over different fake reasons for suddenly needing that much cash, but every idea sounds made-up, contrived to hide something...which it is."

"Don't worry about it too much, Ma. I have another week to find something. Maybe these guys doing Jolly Roger's neighborhood will screw up again next week. My luck can't stay this bad."

"I kept saying that same thing every time I found out I was pregnant. It can stay bad unless something else changes. Go find a rich girlfriend."

The phone rang. It was Mrs. Glenaugh. My chauffeured arrival had also distracted me from noticing the Glenaughs moving furniture and other belongings out of the Old Lady's house. We heard it would be going up for sale as soon as her will cleared probate, which can take two months or another lifetime. The moving truck was positioned so that things could be carried in without being exposed to the hungry eyes of the curious neighbors. Still, I could see my father and two of my brothers over there, helping them move. I started for upstairs to change clothes and join them.

"Hold on, Jack. She wants to talk to you, in person, before they leave for the storage company. Go over to their breezeway. Don't change, they're almost finished."

I wondered what this was about as I crossed the street. Maybe Mrs. Glenaugh wanted me to paint the house; get it ready for sale? She was sitting on the glider in the breezeway.

"Come in, Jack. Have a seat over there. I want to talk to you before any of the boys come in. Now, listen. Do you know what an executor of a will is?"

"Not exactly, but I think it's the person who makes sure the will is correctly followed. Something like..."

"That's close enough, Jack. The point is, I am the executor of my mother's will. Only she and I and her lawyer know that she made some changes to her will just before she passed away. One change involves you and your mother, Jack. But I can't announce what it is nor do anything stated in her will until the court says it's a legal will. Understand? Unfortunately, getting the court's approval can take some time, months at the least. But I know the will is going to be approved and I know what she would want me to do right now, while her gift can do the most good for your family.

"A gift? I don't know anything about a gift from her. I don't want you to get into any legal trouble..."

"I'm not getting into any trouble by paying you this money for working in the garden." She handed me an envelope with a number of fifty dollar bills in it. I was too confused and shocked to try to count it, which would have been rude; but that's what I usually do when handed money...I count it.

"I just need you to sign this receipt. When the court approves the will, you and your mother will be able to "buy" this receipt back. Only your parents can know about this money. For now, its money you earned working in the garden."

Although I couldn't count the bills just then, I could read the amount of "$500" on the receipt. I thanked Mrs. Glenaugh as best I could, considering my feet wanted to turn and run home. Once there, I gave the envelope to my mother. When I asked her to explain this envelope with my freedom in it, she replied in her other language, Latin: "Nunc Pro Tunc," or: now for then.

"It's also 'now, for the future', in our case. So, you still need a job, you're about to spend your inheritance before you get it. At least you won't be wearing striped pajamas."

DRIVING BIG PINK

It was all mine now--the 1955 DeSoto Firedome, with its huge, Hemi V8 engine, and white leather seats. The car that turned Betty Grable's head at the 1955 Auto Show the way Betty Grable's legs turned men's heads [the big one and the little one]. It was sleek and it was pink with white slashing. But by 1965, pink was weird. Large, two-tone cars were "out." But the 7-8 miles per gallon fuel appetite was forever. I didn't really care. I didn't have to share it with my brother anymore. It was mine now.

The Pink Panther came into our family as a fairly old car, given to my father by one of the guys in the band my dad played in, called the Innovations. This guy, Jim, was a trumpet player with some talent, single, young and bound for Las Vegas; but not in an old pink gas-guzzler. So he left the car to my dad, the piano man and father of seven, who just lost his eight-passenger station wagon to terminal engine failure.

Never kick a gift car in the tires, especially when you're broke and bumming rides to work, but pink? Tough to look at in the morning, but you could put a bunch of kids into a big pink DeSoto...a free, big pink DeSoto. Other positives that offset the car's color problem were its exterior lines and sheer size. It impressed as a huge man-eating shark coming at you, all aggressive and well-muscled. The pink color was there just to fool you that it had pastel manners. It wasn't boxy, like a Hummer; more like a Chrysler 300 on steroids. My dear mother, whose driving skills were hampered by her so-so vision and consequent fear of collisions, needed a monster car surrounding her to feel safe. The color and size of this cruiser ensured that other drivers would see her and give way.

Not that Betty drove much...mostly short trips to the market or church. Her longest journeys were to work and to the district courthouse every four weeks with me and my falsely betrayed friends to have our weekly chat with the juvenile probation officer and deliver our partial restitution for the damages of a "vandalism spree" we went on one day over a span of seven years. The way the judge reckoned it, since we were fingered as the vandals who completed breaking one broken window, we must be the same kids who broke all the windows since the school opened, a period of time when most of us were under ten, and I didn't live in the state. Our dads worked on Saturday's [Probation Day] so the mothers took turns driving their criminal offspring to court. Oddly, another mom drove a DeSoto; but it was red and white; almost camouflaged by our standards.

The car met my mother's needs, but there was no doubt the Pink Power was my dad's boat. He constantly praised it for its smooth ride. You'd think he spent the day at a health spa instead of welding boat trailers the way he would carry on about how great he felt after driving home.

"Want your beer, Ed?" my mom would ask.

"No, thanks. Why? I'm fine. Didn't you just see me hop out of the DeSoto? What a ride! I'm feeling pretty relaxed right now. Maybe later, after you tell me about the bills," he'd reply, looking quite sane. We thought it was just for transportation, but it was apparently a mobile psychiatrist's couch.

No doubt the car was a multitasking machine at a perfect price. As my dad's ride to gigs, it was a perfect "fit", able to pack a complete set of skins, a.k.a. drums, in its cavernous trunk. This feature was practically a requirement because the piano man had no "axe" to carry, so he was expected to help the drummer, who had cases of "axe" to carry. My father didn't complain. It was a weekend job that paid pretty well, and was a far cry from welding. He got to do something he loved and get paid while looking very debonair doing it. Most of the time, he was surrounded by interesting people tying one on in an upscale night club.

Beyond the needed money and the buzz of the stage, I believe he had the emotional motivation of working with other musicians. It brought back good memories of a free and easy time. Even before the War, when he was maybe seventeen, he was in a big band. He continued to play in dance bands after returning from his hitch in the Army Air Force where he saw a lot of misery in China, Burma, and India-- the CBI theatre. Playing out maybe helped him cope with some of that experience by sharing it with other vets in the band. Being part of a musical group often created camaraderie you could depend on to support you. It was a feeling of belonging that a person could come to treasure, and easily come to miss.

After finding my mother to have fun with, and siring a lot of kids, he became a full-time, family man with no time or space for a piano. Eventually, as the years and babies mounted up, he needed another job to support those kids. Truth be told, the fun of hanging with us was wearing off. He wanted a job that would be different from his day job and easy to learn. Playing the piano for money was both. He just dusted off his past skills on an old "player piano" he got somewhere, took a few lessons from a nearby teacher, and he was back in the "Swing." There were plenty of gigs in the days before DJ's and small rock bands.

Near the holidays, my dad left for a gig downtown at a well known, jazz club called, The Gaslight. On the way, he stopped to pick up the drummer and his skins. The job went well. The Bandleader gave every member a little bonus for the Holidays. Customers left in a festive spirit while the band had one for the road. My dad and the drummer, Dick, having to pack the drums, were the last to leave. Once packed up, they jumped in the Big Pink for the drive home. The engine was so quiet, you couldn't hear it idle. My dad moved the on-dash gear lever to "D" and gave the Hemi a little nudge...but nothing...no movement. Then, he gave it a short, steady pedal of engine power...still no go.

"Check your handbrake, Eddie," said Dick.

"It's not on. I never use it," Eddie replied. "Nothing will hold this thing back, so why bother?"

He tried all the forward gears and still no movement. They got out and checked the wheels for a block of some kind, a practical joke maybe. They found nothing. Only "Reverse" remained to be tried. Eddie held his breath as he pulled the chrome lever down to "R". With a slight jerk, the gear engaged and pulled the car backward with smooth, low-revving authority. He immediately stopped and tried the other gears again. She would only play in the key of "R."

"Whaddya wanna do, Dick?" Eddie solemnly asked. "Drive home in reverse?

"Not really, Ed. The cops are all out."

"We can't take a cab with all your skins and you can't leave 'em. They'll be..."

"I know, Ed." Dick interrupted, "Sure as hell they'd be stolen. Pretty easy to pop the trunk. Sonafabitch! But driving the streets in reverse, some cop will spot us in this boat."

My father said nothing in reply. He was thinking.

He was always thinking, running an idea all the way through in his mind.

It's late, it's the Holidays... " said Eddie, "Maybe with fewer cars on the road, and the cops out looking for drunks, we'll get to your place un-noticed."

"And we're not gonna look like drunks, in a pink bomber driving backwards at 2 in the morning? They won't see us? We wouldn't be noticed. Is that what you're thinking, Eddie?" Dick joked.

Always the optimist, my dad predicted police mercy if pulled over.

"If we do get stopped, I think the cop will let us go without a ticket. It's Christmas time, for Chrisake... and it's transmission trouble. Nobody drives in reverse down a street unless they have to. We're not kids on a joyride, Dick."

"I don't know, Eddie. But it's your car and your license," Dick pointed out. "I'll split the ticket with ya if you wanna take the risk. At least we haven't been drinking. But, hey ...you try any of those Mary Jane sticks Sam was passing around? What's he call it...pot?"

"No. Have you heard these guys play after they've smoked that? They think they play better, sound "hip" when they're high, ya know? But they miss key changes, slow down the time We'd all be in different keys if I was doped up. You hear music on a different level when you smoke that stuff, but it doesn't help your performance ...you start to lose focus. And it wouldn't help me drive, especially in reverse. Anyway, I only had one beer, so we'll give this a shot." my dad decided, "We're only going about ten blocks, then over the bridge to your place."

So they drove...no-- backed away, my dad with one hand on the ivory steering wheel and the other across the top of the bench seat-- a "pillow' for his twisted jaw and head. Dick looked out the front, alert for following cars. Dad made the ten- block trip up the hill and across the bridge to Dick's apartment without incident. They unloaded the drums, and brought them upstairs to Dick's apartment where they began to consider my dad's next move.

"What about you, Eddie?" Dick asked, concerned. "I'm home. My drums are home. But how do you get home...seriously. You think you can drive in reverse through East Providence, all the way down Rt.1A, in a big pink Desoto? All those stop lights you'll be hitting; intersections, lit-up shops and decorations on poles all along the road, doin' only 15 to 20 miles an hour, stiff-necked from looking over your shoulder out a back windshield that's, like, 10 feet away? Think about it, Eddie. Why don't you make a call to the wife? Tell her you're stuck and you're staying over here. Get a tow tomorrow."

"I don't know if there's a tow truck big enough, Dick," my dad said in mock seriousness. But he was worried: about the cost of a tow, for one thing. Like most working class people back then, he didn't have a Triple A membership. Tow rates had no standards. The cost could be whatever the driver thought you had. At other times, the greater your need, the higher the cost would be. Holidays and late hours were always more expensive. My father had money in his pocket from the gig. Mike Abbott always paid in cash. But he had seven kids...all born a year apart. That's a long Santa's list, even at one present per unit. A tow could cost most of what he made that night. And there were no more paydays 'till Christmas. He did not want to make a call to my mother, telling her: "I'll be home tomorrow... with no money for presents and the car is in the garage."

Eyes closed, he slowly shook his head "No. Thanks" at Dick, who understood that meant Eddie had no choice he could afford. So they had a coffee and a smoke; shook hands and wished each other a Happy Holiday. It was time to move the St. Joseph's statue, with its mystical protection of travelers, from the front dash to the rear deck.

After Dick waved g'bye, my dad "put his mechanic's hat on", which is common shorthand for the male brain shifting into a different and distinct persona to fit the problem at hand. The brain also narrows down to finding and using data only for the emergency. In this case, shifting from "musician guy" mode to "car repair guy" mode; and directing all conscious brain power to whatever that mode required.

Male brains seem adept "locking on" in this manner. They store their knowledge and feelings in well-defined, mental "boxes" they've arranged in their heads. There is one for each kind of knowledge and experience [some like the term, "compartments" over hats or boxes]. Whatever term you prefer, they all provide an image of the divisions created to keep the colors in the paint tray from running into each other and causing confusion. Red stays red, blue stays blue and, so, when you want blue, blue is exactly what you get, and not deep purple. Everything is in its place where a guy can depend on finding it. Downside is, if you get really good at this separation, you'll never discover a neat color like purple, or how your career is important beyond paying bills. Organizing the conscious brain this way ignores that, in real life, things tend to dribble into each other, lines are often blurred and not everything can be fit into only one "box".

In this jam, compartmentalizing was useful. It allowed my father to shut out the dismal facts of his other problems and concentrate on how to prepare for the difficulties of driving backwards for miles at night in reverse gear. Except that it's illegal, what are those actual difficulties? What does a car do differently, or not at all, when moving in reverse?   To answer this, so he could avoid bad surprises, he had to call upon his years as an airplane mechanic, flight inspector, and his auto mechanic's training.

The first safety issue is the loss of brake lights behind you. The driver ahead of you might look in the rearview mirror and see brake lights, but that doesn't help your followers. My dad knew the hand signal for "Stop," but his arm out the window would be hard to see at night; and he needed it to steer. Even if he could do it, the signal just looks like a guy getting the ashes blown off his Lucky Strike.

Another problem is fatigue caused by driving with the head turned around, almost 180 degrees. This quickly makes your neck stiff and narrows your field of vision. Your body has to twist into an uncomfortable position that can make it harder to finesse the brake pedal. Hopefully, you're driving an automatic, or have long legs if you also have to reach the clutch pedal for stops without stalling.

The most fundamental differences in a car's performance are that it would lose speed, stability and normal handling. While moving in reverse, the car loses the help of stabilizing parts and messes with the design that is made for driving forward. An important element of the design is a condition of the front wheels called "caster". The front wheels are deliberately set farther apart at the bottom than the top. This makes the front tires slightly wider apart where they touch the road. So as a driver turns the steering wheel, the tire wheels turn in a wider arc, providing greater control of the car's weight. In reverse, the rear wheels are now in the front; they are straight up, rigid in turns, and have a narrower track than the tires in the rear of the car. The car's weight can quickly shift too much to one side while turning, causing severe body lean and difficulty straightening out when the driver wants to stop turning.

Ever try pushing a loaded shopping cart backwards around a grocery store? If you have-- it's something like that. If you haven't, put it on your shopping list.

Now that my father had his Mechanic's Hat firmly on his head, he walked around the Pink Power with an eye for how it would appear to on-coming vehicles and vehicles behind him. He saw that the clear lenses of the "back-up" lights were large enough to be mistaken for headlights by an unsuspecting driver going in the opposite direction. He was going in reverse, so they would be on, shining brightly, making the rear of the car look like the front. Good deal! On the other end, the front grill could not be made to look like the rear of the car -- no red lights at all.

Having no brake lights would be a major safety flaw. This was giving my father pause. Not that he was afraid to take the risk. What was fundamentally out of character for him was knowingly breaking a law, or any rule he had agreed to follow. Only once before, when he was a ten year-old altar boy, had he deliberately broken a rule by climbing to the top of his church's bell tower. This was forbidden by the pastor, and punishment was strictly enforced for using the narrow, winding stairs that went straight up to the grandest view of the lower Blackstone River Valley any building had to offer. To be able to scan so many miles in all directions was a sensation he had to experience. It overcame all fear of harm, punishment, and shame. Here, he had less choice, and the prize was not fulfilling a rare, self indulgent quest. Nevertheless, following the rules was a fundamental part of his self image, and he had to push that aside before he could start the ride.

He took a moment to remind himself to approach the drive roughly one telephone pole at a time... all eight miles, twenty-six traffic-lights, and two-states of it. Occasionally, he would scan ahead, but he had to remain focused on small distances, stay in the first lane, and avoid the gutter. It was a challenge that called for a "Steady Eddie" at the controls.

"A few bystanders, even a cop, might have to imagine there's a tow trucks pulling me, but I'll get home on these wheels by morning," he promised himself.

This would not be an easy promise to keep. There were no cassette or CD players, not even FM radios in 50's cars, to keep him awake. The only music radio was AM, and the only broadcast after midnight was a modern jazz program. That was right on. He loved his jazz, especially Oscar Peterson, Bill Evans, Errol Garner, and Miles Davis. And though a bit too mellow to keep most people awake, this style of jazz would keep him alert while listening for innovative chord changes. On the sleepy side, the early morning disc jockey had a voice as low and as comforting as James Earl Jones on 'ludes.

The phone poles went by, marking sections of densely packed tenement houses, grouping small businesses, measuring playgrounds, intruding on the images of graveyards and churches. It was a straight ride once he got out of Providence and into Pawtucket. Here he began driving on the four lane interstate, Rt.1A, or

Newport Avenue, as it is also called because it has connected Boston, Massachusetts to Newport, Rhode Island since colonial times. Eddie wasn't Paul Revere on a midnight ride, but he was going about as fast as Paul's horse and his odds of escaping the authorities were about as slim as Revere's were.

He was almost halfway home, and definitely into the groove of driving ass-frontward. All the traffic lights he passed through were just "blinking yellow," which saved time and the need to come to a stop, which would make his car's position much more obvious to anyone in sight of it. But then he came to the big, four-way, fourteen-lane light at Narragansett Race Track, a large jewel in the crown of Eastern, U.S.A. horseracing.

"The goddam light's turning red," he lamented, "And there's the corner Dunkin Donuts. Where's the cop?"

Eddie finally had to stop. While at the red light, he stretched and rubbed his neck. He began to think a coffee and doughnut might be a good precaution against falling asleep.

"I'll have to park sideways in the parking lot behind the coffee shop so I can get out of the lot when I'm ready to leave. Don't let me forget," he warned himself.

Eddie entered the coffee shop and, looking around at the other customers, saw he was a bit over-dressed in his long overcoat and tux, carrying a briefcase full of music he couldn't leave in an un-lockable car. He decided to sit in a booth after he went to the counter and got his cup and a jelly-filled. After a few sips he felt he needed to return some water. Now he was doubly glad he stopped. The coffee and doughnut gave his energy level a needed boost and his bladder a needed drop. Taking the time to stretch out his legs and relax his arms and eyes were not on Eddie's original agenda, but it was a welcome opportunity to let his blood flow freely again. Despite his predicament, he was getting comfortable in this booth, feeling equally prudent and lucky to get this far.

The truth was, my father could find a comfort zone just about anywhere. As my brothers and I got older and started to work with him on cars and repairs around the house, we were amazed at how he could work in a hot, cramped attic; or in a damp, buggy crawl space; a high, slippery rooftop in a storm; or outside in a freezing blizzard without any bother or upset. He'd just get used to the scene and even get to like it. Consider the crawl space job, for example. We had a mysterious hissing noise in the piano room. It seemed to come from under the floor. So we crawled in [how else?] through an old door in the house foundation to find a pipe running under the piano room floor in the crawlspace. It had burst midway across, forming an 8 foot "grotto', 2 feet deep. You couldn't stand up in this part of the cellar, only crouch around like the Hunchback of Notre Dame. It was damp and cold, even in August. There were plenty of bugs flying, crawling and in webs. Evidence of mice was all over the area. Halfway through the plumbing repair, it was time for lunch. My brother, Bobby, went for sandwiches; I for beer. We came back and called dad out for a break. His response: "Aren't we gonna eat in here? It's not bad and it's cooler than outside" Bobby and I looked at each other in disbelief. We should have known.

"Sure, dad. it's a great picnic spot. But the cave is only 4 feet high; there's only a naked droplight to see by, and water is spraying in all directions from the corroded pipe. We're wondering why they don't bring this earthy ambience to fine restaurants." His quaint affection for "going native" was always good for laughs, even if you were totally sober.

90

We found it odder that he never swore at bad news about broken or lost things. For most guys, that's the first thing they do. Then get madder and start blaming other people, and curse their bad luck. Instead, he would take the problem into his life without judging it, or himself, or you, for having it. He saw breakdowns as natural setbacks that happen to teach us something...maybe test us. Whatever the problem, he had always seen worse, would never get discouraged or panic and somehow made it through, made it function, even if not perfectly.

One day while helping a student in my library, I learned that, in French, our last name meant "a war horse that was steadfast in battle." He didn't get the connection.

"Our name stands for a kind of horse?" he questioned me, and was not impressed.

"It can also mean 'fortunate, wise, or happy, as in the Prudhomme spelling, like the chef, a Happy Man," I added. He preferred that definition. He lived as both.

Eddie was always in the moment, and now the moment was 2:46 a.m.. Still, what was the hurry? His experiences in the war, witnessing death, misery, and poverty, taught him that life is found and lost right where you are, not at some other time, in some other place. He survived to appreciate even the smallest pleasures wherever and whenever he found them. Eddie was enjoying this challenge, but knew he had to travel twice the distance already covered before reaching home. Once there, he'd be happy to have ducked the towing costs, even if his neck would be stiff for a week. Eventually, he accepted that it was time to start again.

He slid out of the booth, paid his bill, left a tip, and walked out the front door, half expecting to see the Pink Power parked out there. Then he quickly remembered why it wasn't in the first row. He discretely turned left, and walked along the side of the building toward the rear lot. There it was, all alone, ready to take him home. A large shadow passed him. It was a black and white, pulling into the lot and parking across the front of the DeSoto. Now there were two reasons he couldn't drive forward. A flashlight scanned the car's interior. Suddenly, a spotlight was in his eyes. Eddie heard a door open, then slam.

"Stay where you are, sir," the voice commanded, "You driving this vehicle, sir?"

"Yes, it's mine," Eddie replied, holding a hand up to block the light's glare, "Is there a problem, officer?"

"That's what I want to find out. Why did you park that way? It looks like you were planning to leave in a hurry... get away quick. What's in that briefcase, sir?"

"Music. I mean sheet music, officer. I'm a musician...on my way home from a job in Providence."

"Walk over toward me, please...slowly. Put the case down on your trunk, and then take a couple steps back, he instructed, "Good...stop there. Is the case locked?"

"No. It's open. You can look inside."

"Where's your-- what do you call it?--"axe?" the cop asked, "I don't see an instrument."

"I don't carry my axe. I play the piano. The axe is provided wherever we play, tuned or not. The case will

92

open right up. I'm only carrying it with me because I can't lock the car. If someone stole it, I'd be out of a job."

The cop slowly opened the briefcase. He moved one hand through it while shining the flashlight on its contents: a large ring binder filled with copies of music; sheets of handwritten music, more music, music and...more music; sheets and sheets of music. Then he spotted a commercially printed score of "The Tender Trap," with Frank Sinatra's face on the cover. The cop liked Sinatra, so he opened it. He found more than music.

"Well, well, what we have got here?" he paused, smiling to himself, then at Eddie, "Step over here, please. I want you to see this. I want you to see this just where I found it. No plant. No joke intended, either."

Eddie walked over to look in his case. He expected to see a gun or a small bomb...no particular reason, but what else so alarming could fit in a briefcase All he saw was a gnarly looking cigarette in the middle of the Sinatra music. "Wait! That's a...a tube – no, a stick? It's some kind of marijuana cigarette! How'd it get there?" He said nothing aloud—just stared at it in shocked silence.

"Is that a reefer cigarette?" The cop asked as though he wasn't sure.

"I honestly don't know, but whatever it is, it is not mine. I only smoke cigarettes—Luckies."

"If it's not yours, then what's it doin' in your possession, sir?"

"I don't know how it got in there. Like I first said, I just finished playing at The Gas Light, downtown. It's a busy joint, especially this time of year. Anyone can come

93

around the piano when we're on a break. There's no security watching over anyone's stuff. So, ya know, someone could leave something or drop a stick of whatever that is in my music. When I'm moving music around, I wouldn't notice if something was inside a folded set unless someone called for the tune and I had to open it."

The cop thought about the situation from the point of view that it was 3 a.m., and close to the end of his shift. The guy looked and acted too straight to be high. Then he thought about the Hippie go-go dancer at the Log Den. She might appreciate this little Christmas present more than the sleeping guys in equipment running the evidence cage at HQ. He also knew The Gas Light was a mob joint. This guy might have friends there that would not appreciate a bust with their name in it. Nevertheless, he had to go through the motions, in case someone was watching.

"I need your driver's license and registration, please. Thank you. Hand it out the window to me, please." the cop instructed, thinking to re-start this police interview at the usual beginning, "Maybe this guy is up to something, or the car's hot...no, nobody steals a big, pink DeSoto." Everything checked out clean.

"I'm Officer O'Brien. Here's your briefcase, minus the cigarette. This didn't happen. Right, Mr. Prowse? Have a Merry Christmas." O'Brien turned and got into his cruiser.

Eddie breathed a sigh of relief, but he couldn't drive up to the intersection in reverse.

"Cops usually leave first. He's still in front of me. Well, at least I can back around him, but then what? I'd better stay here 'till he pulls out."

The cop waved for him to back-up. Eddie had no choice; he'd just go slow and...

He hit the brake. There was blue light flashing all around him and then a loud siren blasted as Officer O'Brien sped out of the lot, turning hard for Newport Avenue, fishtailed through the big intersection and headed north to some emergency.

"What luck!" Eddie thought as he backed out and returned to the big, empty intersection "on green" and turned north, as well, "It's been one thing after another; but, so far, it's all turned out my way."

Again he was settling into pole-to-pole travel at a good, safe speed. Then a cop flashed by him at high speed. A few seconds later, another cruiser whizzed past him. This one was a State-y.

"Maybe they're all going where O'Brien went. They sure don't want me. Must be something big. Just hope nobody's hurt," he thought as he looked over to the St. Christopher's statuette. He was now quite alone on the road, heading toward the last the bridge at the state line. From there, he was Massachusetts's problem and could follow the swamp roads the rest of the way home.

Eddie was now rounding the turn before "Eileen's Lodge" and the bridge. Ahead, he could now see a blue, red, and orange glow.

"Strange," he thought, "Even for "Eileen's it's late for the Lodge's party lights to be glaring."

It had the look of an old roadhouse; a place where divorcees and soon-to- be divorcees mingled in song, dance, and cheap drinks until the wee hours. The owners still held a license for overnight lodging. It was, in title and deed, a lodge. So they also had a license to serve liquor until 2 a.m., except Sunday. If you got too drunk or just lucky, they had rooms for rent. This was not Las Vegas, but it was Rhode Island.

Often, rollicking good times have a sad end. This was the case that night. Two cars headed in opposite directions tried to use Eileen's narrow, semi-circular front entrance at the same time. The cars smashed together, and then bounced into the first lane of Newport Avenue, where a car heading north slammed them. This is what Eddie saw the police responding to earlier. They were still there, loading injured. There were no EMT vehicles or fire truck responders in those days—police got to the scene first, then the ambulances.

The Pink Power hardly got any notice, except from Officer O'Brien, as it reversed by the scene. A few heads turned in disgust, thinking it was a disgrace to show such poor taste by goofing around at a scene of pain and serious injury. Eddie felt pretty badly that he couldn't stop and help, but this was his golden opportunity to slide on by, over the bridge to home.

He made it home, with all four wheels of the car on the road. The next day, he slept late. Mom took us to Sunday Mass. After dinner, we all heard the story of how Dad drove all the way home, backwards, in the Big Pink. Later that day, my father saw brother Johnny rummaging through the music case with a distraught look on his face.

"What do need in there, Johnny?" his father asked him. "All your Classical and Rock is in the piano bench."

"I couldn't find what I wanted in the bench. I thought maybe Ma put it in the case. Guess not."

96

"I almost got arrested with that crap in my music..." My father's anger was rare, but rising at this point. The ruse was up.

"If it wasn't in there," Johnny interrupted, "You would'a been busted for driving backwards. The cop took my dope and let you go. You're lucky I put it there. You should thank me," He said as he hurried for the door.

My father just stared at Johnny as he walked for the front door. "That's Johnny Logic, Ed," my mother sighed, shaking her head, holding back a laugh.

"Johnny Logic? It's backwards logic, Betty. Reversed thinking is what it is. And where does he get this..."

THE FLAMING, FLYING SOFA
OF SUFFOLK STREET

If Opportunity knocks only once, and the Postman always rings twice, then how many warning blows do Firemen lay on your door before splitting it in half? The answer is: three, followed by one clear shout to "Open up!" My friend, Dave, and I learned this on a sunny, cold day in the first week of April, 1969, compliments of a few large firemen crowded at the hall door of Dave's third floor apartment. Luckily, we shouted "Wait!" after the "Open up!" and Dave twisted the door handle open at the final second. Once he pushed the door open, the raised axes were slowly lowered to the floor. The firemen looked disappointed.

"Zat your sofa in flames out there on the street?" the fire lieutenant shouted from behind his two axmen.

"No, it's his roommate's," I jumped in, as Dave seemed shocked by the unexpected arrival of city personnel. He had called city hall many times about the sewer backing up and over his toilet. No one ever came to see or fix that emergency.

"You a fuckin' comedian?" The boss asked me, "There are pieces of a burning sofa all over the street in front. A neighbor saw someone throw a burning sofa off that porch!" he gestured toward Dave's third floor porch & trash depository with the big thumb of his thick glove.

"Well, yeah, it came from there. But it's just not technically our sofa. We want to be clear about that," I tried to explain.

"Who cares who owns it? It was thrown from there, right...Anything else on fire in here?" the fire lieutenant demanded to know.

"No. Nothing else," Dave replied."

"I wanna know why you morons set the sofa on fire and threw it into the street. And if someone else tossed it, where is that person? I'm not waiting long. What happened college boys?"

"We don't really wanna say because we don't really know how it caught on fire. We didn't light it, and we don't know who or what started the fire," I said, trying to say as little as possible without getting the lieutenant pissed off.

"OK. Forget the "who" for now. Why didn't somebody here call us? Were you just gonna let it burn down there, waiting for the kids in the school across the street to get out for the walk home? Maybe they could improvise something with the burning pieces?" He looked closely into our faces, almost smelling us. "You guys stoned already?"

"No, we're studying for exams. We are juniors at RIC [one of three local colleges]. We only had a beer," Dave explained, "not even a full glass. We used almost two full quarts trying to put out the fire. Now we're out of beer."

The firemen just stared at us like we were from another culture or time that didn't care about the safety of school kids, or property damage. All we college scum cared about was avoiding the draft by taking classes, passing exams, and getting good enough grades to stay in college... diploma optional. That's what the faces of these firefighters said. They wanted plain answers to account for what they believed was negligent, maybe criminal, mischief that could ultimately cost us our financial aide and federal loans for tuition, and most importantly at that time: Student Deferments from the draft. The Lieutenant took out a long, narrow pad and a sturdy pen.

"Let's start with some simple questions."

He wanted the basic info on us for starters. Later, he wanted to know all our activities that day, not in essay form, but in a timeline. Even his seemingly simple questions were difficult to answer the way we, as college students, were conditioned to answer questions. For one thing, we are expected to present background information before getting into direct discussion of the question at hand. That is the academic protocol. The fireman didn't like this approach. He dismissed it as a wiseass attempt at obscuring the truth, avoiding the question, and stalling—wasting his time. And that was something guilty people do.

Another annoying habit of the academic crowd is a hesitancy to answer questions requiring exact names, numbers, times, or dates, etc., when clarification is needed before a complete and accurate answer can be given. A question such as "When did you leave?" for example, could have many valid responses, prompting questions on our part. When did we leave where? The porch? The apartment? The driveway?

The boldness of young people, who've been in school for 80% of their lives, truly annoyed the fireman. It was another example of not answering, but questioning, authority. You could sense the frustration in the boss's voice and body language. He asks a question he thinks has one answer, and we respond with only more questions for him. The Lieutenant's conclusion is, again, that this is stalling and evasion; therefore, lying. He decided to shake us up a bit.

"You may be interested in knowing that if you're found guilty of arson or malicious mischief from this incident, a lot of things can change for you boys. You may be kicked out of college. Yeah. College boys to jailbirds, just like that" and he snapped his fingers, "But don't worry too much about jail time, because now the judges offer Viet Nam as an alternative to jail. Nice to have options, huh? It's like a 'multiple choice' test.

He came right out and threatened us with what we knew could happen in this situation. It was a tightrope for us to walk. Fail to directly answer the lieutenant would get the police here—no good-- not in an era when a couple of pot seeds could get us busted for possession. Answer too directly and it could be taken for an admission of guilt...easily the lieutenant's conclusion. We had no alternative account, only our assertion that we didn't start the fire.

There was no way the fireman would let us huddle up and get our strategy together. But it was obvious to us that the time had come for Dave and I to answer their questions the way they wanted them answered, no matter how many holes this would leave in the complete explanation. So, moving right along, we established who we were [I was a married man, and a father, a RIC student and daily visitor on weekdays] where we lived, other domiciles besides here [if applicable], for how long, with whom, what we did, if anything, besides attend college, etc. We repeated that Dave had a roomie, Paul, not present, who was also a student at RIC; ditto his pretty girlfriend, Shelly a.k.a., "Frog Face" who was a daily visitor. We four were here more than anyone. Additionally, there were weekend visitors, daily drop-ins, and, sometimes, horrified family visitors.

Some responses required documentation, so Dave's wallets had to be rounded up from their several hiding places: his bedroom, his car, pants he wore three days ago, his book bag, and the wallet I carried for him when he drank in earnest. Everything was checked for currency and validity. If we didn't have draft cards—go directly to

102

jail.

I was a married-with-children guy, so I had mastered some of the organizational tools that allowed me to sail through the documentation part of the program. This left me some time to walk around while the Lieutenant and Dave went through his collection of leather and paper.

I walked onto the porch, earlier the scene of Dave's heroic action. Looking over the rail, I could see the firemen shoveling the burning pieces of sofa into a neat pile for dowsing. The burn marks in the retreating snow and brown grass took the shape of a "connect-the-dots" marijuana leaf.

"What are the chances of that happening," I wondered. It reminded me that, though we had no beer left, at least I still had the weed...wait! Where was the weed? Where the fuck was it? Lying on the kitchen table? Merged with the mess on the kitchen counter? Maybe it's in the frig, retaining freshness? Or in a shoe box cover somewhere, waiting to be cleaned of seeds? It could be hidden in a number of places, or right out in plain sight. "Shee--it." I had to remain cool, but my brain conjured up future scenes of handcuffs and phone calls from the blood and hair littered hallway of the city police station.

I began to casually re-enter the living room and tried to nonchalantly check-out the usual places we leave the bag or a joint. Potential for a major hassle was high. I had to find that lid, or figure out where it went before the lead fireman swaggered over to us, holding it up, asking, "Who belongs to this?" I started to count up the charges, and the extra punishment we'd surely get for drug activity across from a school.

Fortunately, the kids were all in class when the flaming sofa flew into the middle of Suffolk Street. I'll bet the little punks got a rush looking out the window, watching Dave chuck that plump sofa up and out, over the railing, flames coming off the floating cushions and box frame as it descended. Good thing Dave didn't have hair on his chest or he would have lost it. We laughed at the time it was all happening. Now, it seemed like a desperate moment and a radical course of action...more dangerous than wasteful; though we did lose a sofa, all our beer, and maybe our freedom for a while. We could have caught on fire, as well, I guess.

The immediate problem was how to hip Dave to this hidden landmine. Hopefully, he had put my lid out of sight, even if it was on him.

"Okay!" announced the lieutenant, "Now that I know a little about you, Dave, and you ... Groucho," [I always got that with my "mustache glasses" face and size], "let's see what's next."

"Jack. My name is Jack, sir", I corrected him as he reviewed his notes.

"I'm Lt. Moroney. These men are Fireman DiRuzzo and Fireman Osborne. I need to prepare a report on this call. On its face, it looks like some kind of malicious damage to property. So ultimately, this may become a police matter. The police would question each of you separately, but I'm gonna question you two together for the fire report. Why? One: I don't have much time, and two: I don't think either one of you knows how to concoct a consistent lie", he stated as his eyes scanned the kitchen for a chair that didn't have junk, or worse, piled on the seat.

With a jerk of his head, he led us through the

decaying, French doors to the cold, littered living room. Here, at least, we had old stuffed chairs to sit in, though Dave and I had to share a loveseat. At six feet and 230 lbs., Dave "The Hulk", Durand [as he was known to his friends], tipped the cushion enough that I rose about four inches in sitting height. I fought against sliding down the vinyl covering into Dave's body, though it would be an opportunity to ask him about the weed. Just the same, it wouldn't look good if I took that opportunity to whisper something in Hulk's ear.

"Before we start," I said "I need a drink of water or something." I pushed off the loveseat, and turned to face Dave. "Where's the pot?" I whispered in a monotone inhale of breath, "Anyone need a drink of something?" I said as I turned to the firemen.

"No, nothing, Frank." Dave replied, signaling he had not seen it around, or put it anywhere he could remember.

"We're all fine here," Moroney spoke for his crew, "Make it quick."

What I "thirsted" for was an excuse to go over the kitchen in search of the potential evidence. Using my acclaimed peripheral vision from years of CYO basketball, I glanced over all exposed surfaces, silently checked under the books, newspapers, and inside pizza boxes--nothing. I peered into the bathroom, one bedroom, and the pantry. Nothing. I returned without a glass of water. Moroney noticed. I could tell by the way he looked at my empty hands.

"Sorry for the delay, guys. Couldn't find any clean water glasses." I said.

"No shit?" the big fireman smirked, "Providence

water sucks anyway, Groucho. Have one of these flat beers from last night. Or are these ashtrays now? Wanna find out?" he laughed, handing me a half-empty Bud can that was sure to have marinating butts in it.

What a fuckin' ball buster he was. No matter. Now I was pretty sure the lid wasn't lying around in the open somewhere in the kitchen area. And it wasn't in here, unless one of the firemen was sitting on it.

"Let's get right to it," Moroney started, "Where the hell were you dopes all morning? I say you were here, getting drunk, getting high, getting bored. So you decided to stage your own little anti-establishment protest and begin the revolution with a flaming sofa. No doubt you had other things to set ablaze, but someone saw you and called us to the scene before your fried brains could respond. That sound about right? Did I leave anything out? "

Davie knew the reason for throwing the sofa over the railing better than I, but since he was more a reader than a speaker, I began the explanation of our activities that morning:

"Dave and I are in similar majors, with the same basic requirements, so we went to register for fall classes together. That was around 8:30 this morning. Paul and Frog Face were gonna bring some coffee, donuts, and Marlboro Menthols for Dave before we left, but they were late. So we had our usual Breakfast of Champions: English muffins saturated in butter and a cold beer. We wanted to wait for the cigs, but you can't be late for registration. Well, you can, but you'll lose the advantage of being an upper classman. We get first pick for classes from starting time until 10, when everybody comes in and the chaos level peaks.

"Make it short, Groucho. Think 25 words or less, Okay?"

"I'll try, but it's complicated. There are courses you need to take in the same semester that conflict in meeting times. Some courses are only offered in the spring; and some courses have pre-requirements. There's a maze of hurdles to jump. Even for upperclassmen, getting into the right classes to finish a four -year degree in four years is very difficult at RIC.

Then there's the process of registering. You plan at least a year ahead, but you end up with a shaky pyramid of required and elective classes across five or more subjects, and then get in a long line of other upper classmen who also need many of these same classes. If you're lucky, there's a seat for your ass when you get to the head of the line. If not, it's like an orange is pulled out of your pyramid. You try to plug in an alternative class from your second choices. This works if that class is open. If not, another orange is pulled out and the big slide to the floor begins, leaving you at square one.

Dave and I both lost crucial pieces to our carefully designed puzzle very early in the contest. We decided to leave right away and not join the growing mass of sobbing, frustrated students forming in the middle of the gym floor. It's bad for your mental health. Instead, we went to LiquorRama, to buy quarts of Bud [cheapest price/ounce container]. Then to Sal's Lounge for the early lunch special and draft beers. We were steeling ourselves for the next assault on class registration..."

"Back up the truck, Groucho. How does getting mentally impaired, drunk maybe, help you get the course you already missed? Makes no sense, I actually listened to your crap with an open mind, but you're losing me," Moroney complained.

Then Dave intervened, "Sometimes, the guy who copped your seat hits his own wall when a "must have" class closes on him. So he has to get another section of the "must" class, but he can't 'till he drops one or two he already has, because you can only have seven courses on your plate at one time. The course that guy has to cut loose can be the same class you needed, and now it's available, though it wasn't when you were first standing there to sign up for it. You dig? By going away for just the right amount of time, you can return to score the re-opened classes, bing-bing-bing. So..."

"Okay, got it," Moroney interrupted. Maybe he learns better from other, big Irishmen---as opposed to us Groucho types, I thought.

"But courses don't set sofas on fire," he grinned over at DiRuzzo and Osborne, and then turned back to us. "I now have more reason to believe that getting closed out and leaving to get fortified resulted in setting the sofa on fire. Try this: returning to the college and getting some, not all, of what you needed, was enough to screw up your semester. So you came back here to cry in your beer. The more you drank the more you felt like taking your frustrations out on something. So you light up the sofa, pick it up and over it goes. After the laughter, it's naptime and you both leave the sofa to burn on the street right in front of the school.

"How do I say this without offending you, Lt. Moroney," I began "We just don't do something like that, no matter how well your theory fits the facts you have. You probably don't know this, and care even less, but college students get screwed over on a regular basis: teacher doesn't like you so you get a C on an essay exam that you know you earned at least a B. Or a teacher puts you in a group project with some do-nothings who leave

you all the work to do or face a collective "Fail."
Sometimes, even a teacher that actually likes you adds
up your four A's and one B and gives you a final grade of
"B, because it is mathematically correct that 20% of the
time you got a"B." There are no + or − grades here.
Then, if you consider it's only our future on the line, a job
in your field, getting into grad school, or failing you end
up in 'Nam, you can see that college isn't all fun and
games. There's money and years of debt on the line just
to be in college.

"Those administrators ought to be shot for what
they put you poor guys through. Really, I'm close to tears,
Grouchy," Moroney mocked me.

"I'm just saying, sure, there's pressure to succeed.
That doesn't mean we let the college bull shit get to us.
There would be broken statues all over the campus if we
cracked that easily. Professors on crutches would be
blocking the walkways. All the furniture in here would
have flown out long ago. But that is not the case because
over the semesters, all students, even Dave and Groucho
have learned to deal with it. Take it in stride. Act out
and the game's over—you lose. Now, we can draw a
different picture for you; one that fits all the facts, and is
also true."

"Just give us a minute, guys," Dave said as he
stood, hands in pockets, "You've got some of it, Chief, but,
the sofa just started to flame up while Jack was sitting on
it. We were drinking together out on the porch, drowning
our sorrows a little, like you said, and smoking a cig. But
we had to share one, cuz Paul and Frog Face didn't come
back with the coffee and smokes like they promised. So
we were passing it back and forth. Never put it down; no
ashtrays, saving every drag. Then the sofa just burst up in
flames at the far end. So we poured one quart on it and it
went out. I went back to the kitchen to read and Jack

stayed out sitting on the sofa, studying.

Couple minutes later I hear Jack yell, 'Sofa's on fire!'... And I ran out to the porch. 'It started right up next to my fucking books', he was yelling as he's pouring more beer on the flames. I could see that wasn't going to put the fire out for real, so I got next to Jack at the safe end and we stood it up. The flames came right at us from under the seat. I just knew it was gonna take the sofa and maybe the whole place...so it had to go over the railing. Where else is it gonna go? No fire extinguisher here, no hose up here; no phone...didn't pay the bill. So I got my body under it at a good point and jerked the end up on one of my shoulders. Then I bent my knees for a squat launch and...over it went!" Dave finished with a shy grin.

"We watched it roll in flames as it headed for a safe landing," I continued, because I wanted Moroney to know we tried to follow up, not just let it burn. "Then we went down to the yard to get the neighbor's hose--but it was frozen, it's only April 2nd, there's still ice on that side of the house. We dragged it out, cracking all the way. And when I turned it on, all that came out was a slight dribble. So we went to the pay phone over at the corner market to call for help, but the phone was literally cut off-- gone--just a steel cable hanging there. You can check it out. Came back to tell Dave, who was making sure no one, kids especially, was getting near the burning pieces. We saw the woman across the street on the phone, looking at the fire, so we knew at least the cops were coming."

"She doesn't dig our act," Dave broke in, quite animated. Like last summer, when our downstairs neighbor was having a yard party. I was sleeping out on the grass near the sidewalk, barely blocking the walkway to the front door. They just left me there. I mean, people literally stepped over me. But this woman over there, she's gotta get involved with anything in her view. So she came over here, got our hose and turned it on me until I woke up. She can't mind her own business." This side remark only brought frowns to their faces.

"Well, anyway," I resumed, "we came back up here for our coats and filled pans with water. We were about to go down when you guys started banging on the door. You've been here since then. That's the whole story."

"Except how it started," Moroney pointed out. "The answer may be down there in that pile of burnt sofa," he said as he peered down on the street. "We'll have to sift through it," he decided, "Maybe we'll find something. Need a starter, an immediate cause of the fire before I can complete my report. We'll be in touch. Or the police will be in touch, if we find an accelerant or something else indicating arson."

Dave and I felt a little relieved as Moroney and his crew left the apartment and Frank headed downstairs. We were lucky we didn't get stoned or drunk, as usual, or we would have been looking at a police presence and a thorough search, legal or not. At least Moroney & Co. were gone. Now, I could ask Dave where he thought my lid was. Then a nasty possibility crossed my mind: "What if the firemen find it in the sofa debris?" Maybe Dave forgot he hid my stash from Paul there? Mother! It was out of our control now. I asked Dave if he recalled hiding the lid in the sofa.

"No ...well maybe," was all he could say with certainty.

"I do usually hide it under the sofa cushion," Dave answered despondently, "But I can't actually picture myself doing that today. Paul usually finds it anywhere I put it...the scumbag", he cursed as he sank into the abyss

111

of no smokes, no beer, no pot, maybe jail.

So we went back over to LiquorRama to remedy some of these needs. Dave had to cash a check on the way--we were out of money, too-- so we would be longer without relief. Lack of nicotine and alcohol started Dave up again about Lakey forgetting the coffee and smokes, and what he called the "Coffee Expectation Theory".

"I don't recall that theory in any philosophy course, Dave."

"It's a theory about how it happens that every time someone actually offers to bring you back a coffee from their coffee stop, they will always forget your coffee and you will be more disappointed than if they never offered in the first place. That's because you came to expect to have a cup delivered. But when they offer and you say "Sure, thanks. That would be great," and you just toss it off, that's when they do bring coffee back for you and the donuts, and the cigs..."

The theory attempts to explain that the less you expect, the less you'll be let down. And when it does happen as promised, it's all extra. So get those expectations and desires for free delivery down, man, way down. And when the unexpected happens, great. You are blessed, my son."

"It has a tinge of Buddhism in it, Dave," I said, "Very down-to-earth, but mystical... couple grams of Hinduism, too, like: instant karma for the asshole that forgets to bring back the coffee. You need to write a paper for Dr. Hardial on this"

"Bad karma for Paul, man. We've been too long without a butt and a beer; and being under all that Moroney pressure. We are very much on the hook for the sofa and maybe worse. Time for a Bud."

We returned to the door of the apartment on Suffolk Street with arms full of cig cartons, quarts of beer, coffee and French crullers. Dave dropped his keys when he stepped into the kitchen to behold coffee and donuts there on the table. A pack of Luckies, with matches, was nearby; and napkins with stirrers, sugar packets, too. Dangling in the middle of a string hung across the table's edge was the bag of pot with a note attached. It read:

"Bet you asshole's thought we stole it. Fuck you! April Fool's! {belated}. Signed, Paul and Frog Face."

"Look at that!" I said, "I got it back, with all the fixins! The search is over and it didn't end in that pile of charcoal, thank God." Finally we could feel the handcuffs come off.

"And now we know how it started; but it was his sofa anyway," said Dave.

"We know how it started?"

"Definitely. You know Paul. He smokes out there all the time with Frog Face on his lap, reading poetry. Bet any money he came back after we left, went out on the porch, sat on the sofa with his honey and dropped a live butt in between the cushions and frame while groping her. It took a couple hours for it to get a flame going. Needed a breeze, like a methane filled fart from your ass to get it going," he laughed.

"You are a jerk, but it happens to bedtime smokers that way. I'd like to get this version over to Moroney tonight, but Paul is Mr. Sensitive. It's a story he needs to cop to us before trying to explain it to the good lieutenant.

"And I still hafta take a hit for tossing the thing," Dave lamented, "Moroney will hang me up for that, no doubt. Any frosting you'd care to put on that burnt cake, Mr. Prowse?"

"Definitely. Doc Sipple just covered Teddy Roosevelt's "Bully" attitude in class yesterday. According to the principles in his lecture, you were simply acting presidential. You did just what the Rough Rider said a leader ought to do in a crisis. I'll try to recall it correctly. Okay: 'Do what you can, with what you have, where you are.' That's it. No time to wish for this, too bad I don't have that. Hulk' man, you are the TR of Suffolk Street Beat—with a sofa in flames on an old third floor porch; a wooden house with people on all floors and little kids on the second floor; no working fire escapes, nothing at hand to put it out. Isn't it better for that sofa to burn on an empty street? Only you could have lifted it that fast, threw it far enough from the house. Moroney ought to make you a Junior Fire Marshall. I'll call him from my house."

"No way, buddy. One can of frosting is enough— no calls for medals, please."

"OK...no medals. But you risked catching on fire for the safety of others. And I have the pot as your reward. Let's light that up."

"No tokes for Teddy, Groucho. I gotta set an example."

TENTING IN A TEMPEST

Their five year love affair had the "We Survived the Blizzard of '78'" bumper sticker on it, which implied adaptability and tested strength. But there was no sign of rejuvenation of love in the spring of '78 for my brother Johnny and Caroline's relationship. The summer brought drought without many sunny days. By early autumn their passion tree was losing its leaves without a departing burst of color. Not that this was a shocker. Johnny's relationships with girlfriends and women of acquaintance were always fragile. Stability was not a requirement of his interest, being absent in him. And it wasn't much fun, either. He was divorced after giving stability a try and failing. Though the short marriage did produce a lifetime son, a bundle of wonderment, mischief, and curly hair, the son went with the mother. After a mourning period, Johnny was back on the clubbing circuit, swinging away.

As for Caroline, dubbed Cabbie by my sister's 2 year old, she was only 17 or so and the best friend of our youngest sister, Lizzy, when she discovered first love with Johnny. His honest vulnerability and happy outside/sad inside demeanor, along with his youthful games, musical ability and good looks were just too much for Caroline to leave alone. She was the under-aged one, so it was legally and morally Johnny's responsibility to leave her alone. But Caroline was ready to experience the carnal light show, and Johnny was overmatched. Besides, for a first time roll in the grass she felt safe with him, having grown up all around him.

So they got it on. Johnny experienced his umpteenth rebound; Caroline was in love for the first time. Not a balanced couple in many ways. Who could be surprised they were now parting. Most people who knew them were surprised it had lasted as long as it did: about 5 years. But they were fun years, filled with surprises and discovery for Cabbie, ego building and heart mending for Johnny. Now the balloon ride was losing altitude and we could only guess at the cause. But it appeared she was outgrowing him, or he was finally growing up and realizing he should be with someone closer in age, starting a career or doing something besides entertaining Cabbie and his child-self with non-stop partying, fishing trips, and sex in strange places.

But we, their family and closest friends were thinking of ourselves. We would fight to keep them together. For the moment, we simply felt sad and powerless to formulate some brilliant strategy to rekindle their passion for each other; or at least honor its passing with a happy farewell bang for old time's sake. We may have been selfish in this way, but we did need them to help us cope with the coming loss of one of our most decorated, laugh-producing, love mongering couples.

For sure, we were all fed up with the drag their lives had become: daily fighting, threatening, accusing, and bad -mouthing each other to anyone who would listen. The search for a solution was on everyone's daily agenda, except Johnny's and Caroline's, who were still hung up on wrecking and blaming exercises.

Like most matrimonial and pseudo-matrimonial relationships, the cause of the fighting usually involves money; lack of it. Sometimes it also involves how you get it, such as being a stripper or thief, for example. In this case, Johnny lost his high- paying, welder's job at Electric Boat-- submarine builder for the U.S. Navy. The shipyard was huge. So huge that its parking lot regularly left workers a great distance from their job site/building. Workers would car pool rides from their cars to the Front Gate to avoid a half hour hike. This was in the days just before jogging was invented. Well, Johnny's ride got T-boned in the parking lot by a pick-up truck, sending Johnny off his milk crate seat into the steel wall of his driver's van. His neck was injured just enough to keep him out of work and into a million dollar lawsuit against the other driver. His doctor put his neck in a collar brace. Spies for the insurance company kept him in it.

While awaiting trial, he and Cabby had to survive on Workmen's Comp, which was barely one-fifth of what he normally earned. So, they were hurting for money. Cabby didn't like having to waitress while waiting for the Big Payoff. Johnny was A-OK with fishing, and daydreaming about the Big Payoff. Major conflict resulted after a couple of weeks, involving every item they bought, the car they drove, the lack of new clothes, and so on, until they woke up each day ready to fight. Their future was tied to a trial decision that would not come soon. The end of their relationship was coming very soon.

While time was running out for them, life had to go on for the rest of us. I had just changed jobs and was looking for an old floppy disk that held some important files from my last position. In the search, I came across my wife's once indispensable, now merely legendary, Camping List. Though I hadn't seen it for a couple years, I felt as though I held it just yesterday; its familiar, neatly written lines of items forming two equal columns on a sheet of heavyweight copier paper. Yellowed and smudged, as it was even then, by constant handling in yucky weather by dirty, greasy hands, it still retained a patina of authority that "tried and true" paper instructions possess. I mellowed out just holding it. The List was a worry buster that specified every item needed for a comfortable and fun time living out of a tent for a week or more in the woods or at the beach. Trying to recollect what we forgot last time; attempting to recreate, from memory, the essentials we had to bring for all circumstances was utter folly. If someone suggested "Let's go camping!" the next question wasn't "Where," or even, "When," it was, "Does Carly still have the List?" There was no further discussion of tenting without it in our hands.

This was not just pothead paranoia talking. Preparing for a camping trip on three hours or three months notice, the first fear is that of leaving some absolutely essential thing behind. This "something" would be an item we take for granted in our well- equipped home, but found nowhere in Nature nor the trunk of our crumbling Mercedes-Benz. It was a land mine, planted, forgotten, and waiting to rip our mellow minds to shreds of regret and blame. For to leave camp to get a replacement was a hassle: an hour's ride with smoking brakes down a dark, insanely curved, mountain road to some general store that charged quadruple the items' price at your mega mart back home. Having this perfected list knocked that worry out of the picture so we could get on to the other possible bummers, like having enough money for gas, the weather forecast, the condition of our cars, and whether we could fit everyone in the tent.

But it was all cool once everything was checked off the List. At that point, we were well started for a good time and free to get stoned stupid. We would arrive at the campsite with our shit together, even if it was dark. Whether we had two days or a whole week, it would all go "swimmingly", as the Brits say, and hassle- free once we subdued the Ted Williams tent.

Jim, the droll Park Ranger would greet us just like he never saw us before. This lanky, plain looking, man of no particular age always astounded us with the heavy Ranger chicks he had staying in his tent, like models out of a Playboy "Co-eds of the Berkshires" spread. We'd notice a different Rangerette type shadowing him each trip. Sometimes, there was more than one in our week. Maybe it was his green Scarecrow hat and muddy mountain bike that made him the stud of Greylock. Or it could have been the corn cob pipe. He's probably still there, or his kids are.

Each trip was different in detail, but they were all comfortably exciting; relaxing but fun, and full of the sights, smells, and feel of living in the deep woods. Other people searched out far-away destinations for their vacations, required more amenities, high tech attractions, mini-bars. Not us. We'd rather watch, mystified, as a toad slowly, but surely, hops to its death in our campfire embers. Save him and put him back in the woods only to run over him, hours later, returning from a liquor run. Toad suicide? Bad rescue skills? Destiny? You won't see that at Disneyworld if you show up every day for decades. Comparing others' vacations, we had neither regrets nor jealousies.

Over several years, degrees, marriages, children, and crises we always found a Greylock trip an opportunity to re-connect with our authentic selves. The List in my hands brought those memories back and it occurred to me that maybe Johnny and Caroline's relationship could re-connect there, too, it being their favorite getaway.

So Carly and I, being the oldest couple, called up the regulars, except the couple in jeopardy, and ran the idea by them first. The plan held real promise: it had tradition going for it, adventure, romance by the moonlit stream, and a pothead posse to keep it all cool. The decision was unanimous! Johnny and Caroline would leave their troubles and hurts at home and let the natural harmony of the mountain fill their hearts and heads; open their eyes to the long view of their first coming together and a possible future, a wider perspective on all the things they agreed on, shared, and wanted from the other. We decided on three mutually do-able, four-day weekends. Then somebody rolled a joint, Kathy opened a bottle of

Mateus, and Wayne put on some Van Morrison. I put Lil' Rodney in his candy cane pj's and off to bed, while Carly called Johnny and Cabbie over for some partying and trip planning. Its larger purpose, we kept secret.

The idea of a love rescue on Mount Greylock was a bit ironic, because the mountain campground was discovered for us by Johnny's old girlfriend and later, ex-wife, while she was away from Johnny to become a lonely frosh at Westfield College. All frosh were required to live on campus in shared rooms. Johnny was hundreds of miles away. So when he could afford the gas to get up there on a weekend, they had to make the most of it. The college was only about 10 miles from the mountain, which was known to the locals and college kids as a good place to get buzzed, do the groove thing "al fresco," and check out the sunset. It became their first pad together, even if it was the inside of a "Ted Williams" tent.

The outside had a mountain in the front yard and a gurgling stream in the back, providing a major head and body trip that would bond lovers together tighter than going to a movie, followed by hop-to-it, wham-bam sex in a friend's smelly, off-campus, 3rd floor estate. In spite of this romantic beginning, the magic mountain memories did not sustain their marriage. Would this trip make it 0-2? It was a fair question. But Johnny had gained some maturity over the last five years. We would gamble on them and the mountain.

Our familiar destination had some formal history as well, being the highest point in Massachusetts, the jewel of the Berkshire Mountain Range. The mountain was named for an un-conquered Abenaki war chief, a renowned leader with a distinctive grey streak, or lock, of hair running right through the middle of his mane. Chief Greylock, as the English settlers called him, fought successfully against the English militias well into his seventies. The whites originally named the mountain "Saddleball or Saddle back Mountain," for its general appearance and the ball-shaped formation near the summit. It was later changed to Greylock, it is guessed, to pay him homage and thereby, keep him the hell away. Its shape and size also served as an inspiration to early American writers, such as Melville, [who saw in the humped-back mountain the very shape of his great white whale], Hawthorne, and Henry David Thoreau. With this impressive résumé, the mountain became the Commonwealth's first State Park, and was set aside for protection from the ravages of industrial exploitation.

We liked to think it was saved for us: our counter-culture generation that championed a "back to nature" movement. Most of this generation, including our particular group of eight or so, were in our college/Hippie years and disillusioned with the Viet Nam War, materialism, and urbanization. Greylock was a sacred wilderness, untouched and off-limits to commercial enterprise. It was an intimate and ancient place, magical, even when you were totally straight, that possessed the power to calm the nerves, slow time, and open the mind and senses to Nature's revelations, such as stoned sex under the wary eye of a chipmunk.

But it was not "built for comfort." The campground was constructed for tents, not trailers or early motor homes. Most visitors hiked in to the camping area, which included some log lean-to's along the Appalachian Trail, which coursed the ridge of the mountain. Free-running pipes delivered ice cold water near each site. No showers, no sinks, no swimming pool. Outhouses ruled, though some kind of desperate animal chewed on their wooden seats. So you didn't spend much time sprucing-up for the day. That left more time for wood-grilling Spam and looking for matches. Electricity was not to be found except at the Summit, in the hikers' lodge, where there were also potato chips and candy. It was rustic, and meant to stay that way. This did not please most tourists, which was a pleasant side-effect.

On this mountain we played, laughed and loved until we hurt. Then later recalled most of what happened. But unlike many memories that were common to several places and challenged us to recall which beach that was, or whose cabin we visited, Greylock behavior and incidences would only happen there, only be that funny there, had a context there. It's similar to the notion expressed in those ads that start: "what happens in Vegas..." and if you've been there and done that, you know what that means. Our version of that was "only on Greylock." The phrase would immediately pre- confirm what we were about to say as "true and unique" to anyone who has tented on Greylock for more than a weekend.

As we recalled the mystery and strength of good times there, our confidence grew in the ability of our plan to get Johnny and Cabbie back on track. Unfortunately, our initial enthusiasm for making the trip began to falter before we even met to divide up the items on The List, as couples in our group began to drop out. Each had good reasons: new responsibilities and work hours emerged for one couple; another lost what remained of summer weekends to their kid's sudden interest in baseball; and there were people who had last minute emergencies. By "Go-Day" morning, the trip party was down to just two couples: Carly and me, Johnny and Cabbie. Not a high ratio of rescuers to injured, but the List had been completed, the GMC Suburban, a.k.a. the Blue Moose, was gassed and oiled, and the foliage report was for "peak" conditions on the Mohawk Trail.

Johnny, decked out in a neck brace and new flannel shirt, stopped inhaling long enough to say, "Let's go."

Cabbie looked happy just to sit up high in the truck's back seat, surrounded by so much stuff, she couldn't get out anyway. So we left for the Berkshires, leaving a small cloud of blue smoke behind us.

The sunny ride of morning became more grey and damp with each hour driving northwest. Drizzle came with our foliage by lunch, and the cheery banter began to turn to discussions that turned into long, loud disputes. The weather was supposed to be supportive of our mission, but this was New England, and so it supported slamming shots. We stopped to shop at the famous Price Chopper Supermarket. A giant neon tomahawk points you into the parking lot, once the site of Fort Massachusetts and a battle there with Chief Greylock. It was a windy ride up the steep and slick mountain road to the campground.

The weather was so bad we had our pick of sites, so we went with our original and best choice, Site #3. This site was like a corner condo unit, with no sites around it, a stream right on one side, and a clearing in the tree canopy above us to let in the moonlight [when available]. There'd be no moonlight tonight, just lightning. If we didn't know that tent like the shelf layout of Steve's Liquors, we'd have never beaten the high winds and heavy rain that started as soon as we raised it.

There was no chance of getting a fire going, so we lost our fundamental comfort and distraction from the storm, which was intensifying. Huddled in a damp, swaying tent, with only a flashlight was not what we expected for our first evening. Soon the "shoulda, woulda, coulda's" started.

Carly looked at me like, "This isn't going to be

easy," and she was always the optimist, 100%, right to the brink of certain failure. So I really started to have doubts, but not with the plan, only the parts we couldn't control-- like weather. But after pleading with our couple to keep it civil, reasonable, at least less ear shattering, Carly and I began to realize we couldn't control the damage they were bent on doing to each other either.

"It doesn't sound like the fucking love generation in here! I shouted above them, "We fight, too, but after a while we get sick of it and start fucking."

That's when we felt a steady gust of wind against the tent's skin. Up came a side of floor spikes, reducing the tent to about half its size, the flapping wall hitting us like a wet towel. We quickly decided to get off the mountain before we got blown off.

Good thing we had been drinking because it was no joy lugging soggy paper bags of groceries to the Blue Moose, then chasing tent poles around in the mud and wrapping up the wet tent in a tangled ball of canvas and vinyl that we desperately managed to force through the rear window of the truck, right on top of our bedding. We'd have crashed for the night right there in the truck, but it started rocking with the wind and sometimes sliding forward a bit. So we got out a map and tried to focus our bloodshot eyes on it for routes with lodging. It wasn't fun, and only exciting in a bad way. On the other hand, the continual arguing stopped.

After reaching the main road at the base of the mountain, we began to realize that map information was of little value at this hour. All that mattered was whether the motel had the "NO" lit on its vacancy sign. As we drove along, wet and bumming out, every "No" was lit, and silent disappointment soon turned again to loud accusations. I finally pulled into a truck stop for coffee and

125

some pleasant noise. Carly went with me, leaving the combatants to themselves. We returned with coffee, Vermont cheese, and apples, to a pair of sadly quiet passengers.

We guessed they finally got to the bottom of it, whatever "it" was. We took off our wet jackets and let the truck heater work on our inner layers. To the delight of no one except himself, Johnny removed his sneakers and his signature, white socks and began scratching his feet. He had some kind of psoriasis that flared up when he was nervous or disturbed [which was almost always]. We preferred he just pull on his mustache for comforting.

We headed toward home and a steady line of motel/hotels lying in that direction along Rt.2. Just after the famous "Hairpin Turn" we crested Mt. Whittier and passes a steady line of "No Vacancy" signs. Curiously, the U.S.A.'s oldest roadside cabin business, the venerable Mt. Whittier Motel and Cabins, had a vacancy left! It was a one room, cabin with a porch and a double bed [a queen-size wouldn't fit]. Carly and I went in to take it, with thoughts of sneaking in the Couple with Troubles. But the old guy behind the hazy Plexiglas had seen this trick before, as well as Johnny and Cabbie silhouettes as we entered the driveway. It took some convincing for him to let four of us sleep in a two-person unit. But he could see we were wet and cold, and he knew there were no other vacancies before the interstate, hours away.

We only brought in the essentials for getting stoned, drunk and getting up. Our foursome was wiped out, yelled out, and smelled out, thanks to Johnny's feet. As hoped, the Panama Red and Yukon Jack nullified the odor, and brought blessed sleep to us. But soon I was ripped from my doze by Caroline's scream.

"Where's Johnny?" she asked as if we might know,

126

"He's gone! He's outside somewhere in the fog without shoes. You have to get him back! Jack, go find him before he gets himself killed."

Johnny without shoes was actually more dangerous to others than to himself. But it was a sign he was desperate. This would be a tough job: we had no "Marco/Polo" locating technique, no GPS, nothing but a tired, scratchy voice and a weak flashlight. It was around 3 a.m. and I was standing in the middle of Rt.2, at the highest point on the heavily- traveled Mohawk Trail, in a fog so thick I could barely see my brother sitting at my feet exactly on the double white lines of the blind turn on the two- lane road, expecting a car to come around and make road-kill of us any moment. We were, literally, in a cloud.

But my head and heart were clear about what I had to do, and my gut confirmed it: I had to tell my brother of 28 years that I loved him-- something I had never said to him despite thousands upon thousands of words and sentences I had spoken to him on thousands of topics, under many circumstances.

On finding him here, he had told me that he wanted to die, having nothing to live for and no one who loved him. His beloved Caroline was leaving him for one of his friends. So it was time to end the pain of the past few months and the future pain he knew was coming. He had picked a good place to find death, sure enough. Another car rounded the turn, just missing Chief Sitting Sad. I needed to quickly and forcefully change his heart. All my attempts to put a positive spin on her leaving would not move him. I wasn't powerful enough to knock him out and drag him back to our cabin. I was actually going to have to speak the words, but I didn't feel shy about it. In fact, I felt a bit of pride that I had the guts to say, "I love you, Johnny."

Guts? Yeah, guts! At this time in many hetero men's emotional development, [early 70's] "the three words" were used only in carnal business with the opposite sex. Our own mothers didn't hear we loved them. So, sadly, it was indeed a giant step for the emotionally mute, and a surprised Johnny immediately got to his feet and hugged me.

"You do, Jack?" with tears in his eyes and some hope in his voice.

"Of course I do. You're my brother," I told him, "But I'd love you even if you weren't my brother. Now let's get the hell out of the road before we get run over."

We dragged ass back to the cabin and joined our fearful bedmates. After a few drinks we could finally relax. We even started to laugh about the four of us having to share one double bed; and the look on the old man's face in the cabin office when we practically begged him to rent it to us that way. What the old man may have suspected to be a mix n' match foursome in Cabin #2, turned out to be a chilled, sexless huddling in the aftermath of near disaster.

The next morning didn't bring a continuation of hope and love and peace, but more fighting between Johnny and Caroline. Carly and I knew our attempt had failed. Not even the suicide attempt [does it ever?] could change the course of this relationship. We would think more about the consequences later. For now, we continued to ride out a tenting trip that lacked party numbers; was surprised by a tempest in the middle of the night; got everything soaked and smelly; and would go down in the book as a prime example of how even the best weed, bourbon, and beautiful memories can't save a bummer camping weekend, or a love both people don't share. What was supposed to rekindle their love, instead, blew rain on it for the final sign that it was dead and gone. Not even a roach left.

So it was Sunday morning coming down the mountain for home, when we heard and felt something heavy smash up against the floor of the truck, and then... no power. We were barely an hour away from the cabin, and already another catastrophe. We couldn't believe it could be more bad news so soon. A simple coincidence if you don't buy into the Screenwriter God. If you do, this is another test of faith, a small scale "Book of Job" for modern beginners. Whatever your belief system, it's not advisable to think or say "No way," or "Things couldn't get worse," because they always can. And statements like those only guarantee things will get worse. "What now?" is a better reaction: you're angry, but it shows respect for the enormous, in fact, limitless, supply of unwanted occurrences available in the universe. And owing to this limitless number, they can be expected to happen in a short period of time, so they can all get on stage before the curtain falls on the play, a.k.a., your life.

In our superficial, micro-world of shadows, this was a busted driveshaft. A quick look under the floor confirmed it. But we were actually lucky. The driveshaft yoke broke off [very rare and very bad], but the remaining length of shaft fell onto a cable. That kept the shaft from hitting the road, digging in, and snapping the other end, or possibly snapping a gear in the rear end. Or it could have hit the road and bounced back through the floor causing injuries, ripping out fuel or brake lines. But none of this happened. Only the yoke got damaged, preventing the engine from turning the rear wheels. No driveshaft, no drive.

Nevertheless, we were fortunate. Maybe events were turning toward the positive, this being the transition stage where things get worse, but nowhere near as bad as they easily could have been. Then I remembered it was Sunday. In Massachusetts, with its Blue Laws in full effect in the early 70's, everything was closed on Sunday, except churches. No open service garages. Stores were closed, including auto parts stores. So there was no one to call, even if we found a phone. We were again on the uphill, far from the nearest town and garage on this beautiful mountain.

Great adventure, maybe comfort, at least a solution could lie ahead. But as I looked at my crew sitting in the truck from my seat on the hard, cold toolbox and back again at the jagged edge of the broken-wishbone shaped yoke at my feet, I knew I was a long way from any of those destinations. Maybe I'll have a bowl of self-pity for breakfast. A familiar mode of consciousness began to take charge of my brain: the emotionally detached, physically hardened, problem solver persona. I would get this truck fixed somewhere, some way, and gain more self-reliance from gittin' her done. My passengers would rev me up with their sworn confidence in my skills. Gratitude and praise for my efforts would follow. But the actual process is carried out in a solitary state of mind, accompanied only by fear of failure and injury... to keep you centered.

From past experience, I knew the first steps would be the hardest and the most important for success. I had to accurately visualize the correct order of repair. Then I heard a voice, very much like my own, speaking close to my ear in a tone of solemn confidence. I looked over my shoulder to see bro Johnny on one knee, his face so serious I almost laughed.

"Caroline and I are gonna hitch a ride to that little town where they're havin' a chicken barbecue today. Remember? And we'll get someone to tow the

130

Moose, with you and Carly in it, or maybe they'll just get you guys and some stuff and bring you to us. Then, we'll find a place to stay, and a garage, leave a note where the truck is, what we need, ya know, and go back to the barbecue. I'll find someone there who'll know where we can stay overnight. Tomorrow, the garage will get the part, tow the Moose to town and fix it. I'll tell 'em not to rip you off. No fuckin' rip-offs just cuz we got long hair, don't live around here. Then, we drive home," he explained.

This was not normal. He usually let me handle all the problems and planning, especially those dealing with strangers in their strange land.

"Think you'll get a ride?" I challenged. This was hunter country, not Hippie country. Caroline stepped up, dressed in farmer jeans, a short, pink tube top pointing out from around the jean bib and long blonde hair. She looked like she'd get a ride, but with Johnny the hobo and his decrepit neck brace? The Carly and Cabbie duo was a sure ride, but to where? "Deliverence?" Too dangerous. It had to be Johnny and Cabby. "You better make sure you get in first, or they'll take her and leave you behind." I advised Johnny, "Thanks for doing this. Sure you're up to it?"

"You-are-my-bro-ther," he pecked out like a robot. "You-need-help. We-get-help."

That kind of weird talk was more like the happily strange Johnny. He must have been feeling a little like his old self. I gave them some of our money and they began walking up the hill, turning to "thumb" each time a car approached. Then they disappeared over the crest of the hill.

Carly and I started neatening up the truck, and

131

airing it out, figuring we might end up sleeping in it. And we did. But not before Johnny and Cabbie returned a couple hours later with a tow truck driven by Al, a young local, who worked for Joe, the old guy who owned the only garage in town. All this good luck started when Johnny and Cabbie got a quick ride from a couple headed for the BBQ. Johnny blended right in with the BBQ folk and quickly bonded with this guy, Al, apparently using Caroline as his bait, and convinced him to leave the BBQ on a "mission of mercy" to save us: great parents with two handicapped kids. Al put us on the hook, Johnny and Cabbie squeezed in the cab with Skinny Al, and Carly and I rode facing backwards in the front seat of the Blue Moose. Have to admit it was a new perspective, seeing what you've just passed.

All the same, I came into the town garage feeling as much "on the hook" as the truck was. Night was falling, and I began to feel a certain dread about our prospects. What's this repair gonna cost? How long will it take? Can my mom continue to watch the kids? Will there be trouble about missing work? These concerns don't mix well with smoking pot. It was called "bumming out." There were things to be done, like making phone calls ASAP, but past experience told us to first get it together, have a plan to tell the straight people. Again, it was Johnny to the rescue. He jumped in the truck as soon as it hit the ground.

"It's all set up, Jack," he announced rubbing his hands together in a self-congratulatory way, "I got to meet Joe. He's the owner. An old guy living right over..."

He moved his straight arm around like a needle on a compass, then stopped, "there, up the hill from the service garage. He says we can stay on the lot in the truck overnight, or sleep on their porch. His wife has a garden... I'm going back later to get some tomatoes from

132

his wife. And he keeps bees, too. Honey and blueberries tomorrow. Fuckin' guy loves me, man. I told him: no screwing my bro-ther on this job. We're not paying more than $25 for the tow, either."

Then he says, lowering his baritone voice, "The tow's gonna work out to be free, son. And your brother shouldn't worry himself about the repair. We treat everybody right. Like they was family. And m' wife thinks you're one funny guy," Johnny laughed, trying to imitate Joe's Western Massachusetts dialect.

"Good job, JOHNNY!" Cabbie whooped, hugging him.

Carly and I were also glad to hear his tale of finding a good port in a storm. But we were a little stupefied. Like it 'blew our minds' that Johnny was: 1) Motivated; 2) had positively impressed someone, despite his soggy campfire attire and toilet; and 3) succeeded in reaching a productive agreement on something that really mattered. Favorably impressing important strangers, earning their affection and trust, and getting their help was my forte; my persona; a skill I honed. It got me jobs of pay and responsibility from sixth grade to the present; scholarships throughout college, completing grad school with honors and awards and a nice position soon afterward.

To have Johnny suddenly do "my thing" was a little unsettling, even if welcome for its results. Where did this suddenly come from? Was it a one-time thing just to goof with me or the start of an earth-plate shift, promising decades of continuing movement? These thoughts didn't help my sleep. Neither did the smell of those same socks, mixed with cheddar cheese, whiskey, and cigarette smoke; the hourly alarm from the nearby dam; and a train whistle every 2 hours as it sped through town on tracks right across the street from us. Johnny slept well, relaxing in the deep, replenishing sleep owed to the "Doer of Good Deeds."

The next morning, I awoke to bright sunlight streaming into the truck. Outside was a bright, New England fall day; perfect weather. Where was it yesterday and the whole weekend? Looking out the passenger window, I could see Carly and Caroline getting breakfast organized on the flimsy folding table. The windows were open, so I could hear them talking about blueberries and getting me to light the Coleman stove. I closed my eyes. Maybe I wouldn't have to get up for a little while. Then, Carly's face was at the passenger window.

"Jack? Are you getting up? Caroline wants to use the bathroom, but there's only one and it's in the garage with the mechanics and some other guys just hanging around."

"So?" I replied, "What do you need me for?" I asked, not fully awake and not listening.

"She doesn't want to walk by herself past all those guys in the garage, to get to the bathroom," Carly replied. She left out the "stupid" from the end of her sentence, but I could feel it. I was beginning to get with the scene.

"Where's Johnny?" I asked, "Can't he take her? He should go in, too ... and someone should wash his stinkin' feet."

"Johnny went to Joe's house to get blueberries for our pancakes, but he's been gone an hour already and she really has to go, now."

134

"Okay... I'll try to move. But my right arm's numb, my neck feels broken and my feet are swollen. Got any cold beers left in the cooler?"

I asked as I pushed my fingers through my Hippie-length, unwashed, flattened down, hair. Sleeping in the driver's seat an hour or two at a stretch did not leave me feeling psyched for this hassle, but I managed to pull myself out of the truck so Caroline wouldn't have to float a kidney or walk the gauntlet of 'perv's' by herself.

As we entered the garage, I could understand why Caroline, unafraid of sharing a dark outhouse with an unknown animal, would still hesitate to enter this place-de- toilet. It was not because of a few gawkers. They politely checked her out with one eye while giving me the "long-haired faggot" glare with the other. No, the actual privacy concern was to our left, beyond the tire racks. It was a large, paneled box labeled "Restroom," jutting out from the far wall. Some moron left it topless, without a ceiling over the three outer walls that ended about six feet short of the garage's ceiling. There was a door with no lock, no windows [good thing] and the walls were made of low grade, interior paneling.

Except that there was a sink and toilet in it, you could say it was built as a sound amplification chamber; a large, stinking, stereo speaker pointed upwards at the garage ceiling.

Any noise made in that room would travel around the thin, uncovered walls; off the hard, slab floor; growing in volume as it carried up and out the open top; bounce off the hardwood ceiling and resound throughout the garage for all in the area to hear. Even to release a princess-like pee would alert the garage folk to every stream and dribble, the roll of the toilet paper dispenser, and all your grunts, sighs and moans.

But this room was all there was... and nature was screaming. So Caroline hobbled into the echo box and I stood guard outside the door, hoping a mechanic would start an engine or an air wrench for noise cover.

But instead, all I heard was "Coffffee Mannn!" and suddenly it was coffee break. Now everybody stopped work, including the coffee man, and tuned-in to the unseen, but totally there, tall blonde chick in the box dropping her 'undies' to squirt the bowl. The very same seat their ass sat on was now being sat on by that ass, the one rounding out the jeans they just ogled. It was the quietest coffee break I never heard: no ball-busting chatter, no laughing, no coughing, no loud chewing; not even a radio playing on a tool bench, just absolute, rapt silence.

Caroline didn't allow the situation one moment of hesitation, but started doing what she had to do. I wanted to generate some kind of distraction from her business, but what to do? Clogg dance, lay on a car horn? Then he walked in, playing his harmonica, smiling and shouting,

"Hey! What's happenin', man?" to all in his path as he walked to the door of the box and knocked.

I gave him my most disgusted smirk. But he just smiled at me.

"It's Johnny, Cabby. Cover up the goods, 'cuz I'm comin' in with ya...gotta take a wicked bad shit from eating all those beans and cheddar cheese." Then he went in to crank up his own Dolby sound-a-round. And there would be odor.

The door was now more secure than I or any lock

could make it, so I walked over to the coffee truck, bought four coffees and went back to give Carly the good news on the restroom. If Johnny did his job well, none of the locals would go near that room, nor allow it in their awareness for a couple of hours. Plenty of time for Carly and me to use it before breakfast.

Approaching our little camp, I saw the heaping basket of moist, glistening blueberries sitting on the flimsy table. Carly just finished giving them a good rinse from the nearby hose and the hot sun was starting to dry them off, releasing a sweet vapor into the breeze. I left my coffee and went looking for the stove and a book of matches.

"Have your coffee, Carly, and let's get these little babies in the batter and on the griddle!" I enthused, rubbing my hands, "I'm stahvin Mahvin!"

"Johnny said wait 'till he gets back before starting the pancakes," Carly stated.

"Why?"

"He said he has something else to add into the batter."

"Like what? Where is it?" I was becoming annoyed at this hang-up.

"I don't know," Carly calmly replied, "But he said you'll like it. Just get the stove ready while we're waiting."

Shortly, they came back from the garage, looking all relieved and fresh and happy. Happy? Wait a minute! Their eyes are kinda blood shot...they've been crying. No. They're stoned. Eee Mere! They've been smoking shit in the shit box! No doubt. Except for a possible explosion, why not light up in there? Who could smell anything except Johnny's contribution? But we were out of weed, so he must have found a joint in his clean underwear or something.

"You guys are fucking wasted," I told them, "Where'd you get the joint? Not on the floor in there."

"You gotta try this righteous home-grown, Jack," Johnny said, "You're gonna freak out when I tell you about it! I am pinned, man. Cabby can barely walk. Her face is gonna crack from smiling so wide. Look at it, Jack. Does it hurt, Caroline?"

Johnny asked as he gently tried to shorten her wide grin by pushing her cheeks together.

"You are both fucked up, but Carly and I wanna use the room you just blew up. Get back here, and start the pancakes." I said, "Then you can tell us all about it. Carly and I grabbed our change of clothes and bath kit."

Johnny came over and pushed a fatty into my hand. "Don't do it all in there or you might get lost, brother," he whispered as he handed me matches, "Light a couple for the smell!" he joked.

"Tell me about it," Carly laughed at him, "It's one of the reasons we had to get our own apartment."

"I'll tell you about it. Don't you worry about that, young lady," Johnny replied, slowly nodding his head over and over with one eyebrow arched like some Vincent Price character.

This was the old Johnny talkin to ya: the overtly crazy act, way past not needed. But it made us laugh because we knew he knew it was ridiculous, yet he did it anyway on the chance we'd get it, and laugh at him laughing at himself. Usually this drives us crazy, but it was good to see him return to his normal. I wondered what caused this rise in his sprits. It wasn't the pot. Lately, getting high just made him sleepy or sad. We laughed and left for the dream bath.

They were cooking the ham slices from Price Chopper and drinking beers when we came back. Caroline had mellowed out a bit and we were all finally ready to mix the pancakes. So Carly mixed up the batter according to the actual instructions on the box. That's why we chose her to do it. That's also why she's the one who made up the List. That's her bag. But the adding of other things is what Johnny and I do. First, the blueberries- all done.

"What's the mystery addition, Johnny?" I asked as I looked through the cooler for it.

"Right here," he said as he turned to show us a medium Tupperware bowl, shielding it from others' view.

"Mashed potatoes?" I guessed, "I don't want potatoes mixed with blueberries. Why are you hiding them?"

"Nooo. Not mashed potatoes, Johnny. What do you put in brownies for a special party?"

"Where'd you...wait! Don't put any in yet. I'm starving. Carly and I don't wanna get stoned on an empty stomach, man. Let's make a batch of just blueberry for now."

After we all had a full round of blueberry, Johnny mixed in a few buds from the plastic bowl, rolling them in his hands to grind out the leaf parts into the second batter mix. I checked out the stuff while he whipped the combo batch together. This was bodacious weed to the eye and nose. When you don't know the weed, it's best to respect its possible, ass-kicking effect. So, I hipped Carly to be careful, to wait after the first couple pancakes before having too many. That's what I planned, anyway, because I've had pot paranoia come on me suddenly, especially in a strange place, around people I didn't know.

Besides, Old Joe could come over any time, without warning, and start talking business. I couldn't afford to be stoned stupid while talking to a old straight guy about repair costs. As suspected, two bluepot pancakes were enough to get trés mellow. I felt relaxed and floated to my usual focus when stoned, of music and images in the moment. I forgot all about asking Johnny where the shit came from and how he scored without any money. After another beer, though, my mind returned to the repair job.

"When you were over Joe's, did you think to ask him about the part? Like if he has one or when he can get one?", I asked Johnny, "The truck's still here and no one's come to tell us they're gonna push it in the garage today...unless he said something to you..."

"Well, I'll tell ya, Jack, it won't be today. 'Fraid not, buddy boy. I've been checking it out for ya. Joe had Al call their parts guy and the local dealer, and nobody has a yoke. Another dealer has one, but they're far away and they've made their daily parts run, so we won't get it 'till early tomorrow. Al's cutting out the old yoke later so he'll be ready to weld on the new one as soon as he gets it. That means...you have all day to play wiffle ball."

The idea of choosing to play wiffle ball and let your problems simply pass out of mind is not in my training. I wouldn't say it's not in my nature, because

140

Johnny's and my "nature' are very much alike and he is living the "gone fishin" life. But being the oldest brother, I'm living the other side of the coin, like the Gemini's we are. I was lovingly groomed to be the "big brother". The BB gets lots of attention and gratitude, even some power in the family boardroom for his work and accomplishments. BB gets a good feeling from saving the baby from falling off the table, stopping a brother from cutting a sister's hair off, discovering a fire on the roof, beating up bullies that threaten your siblings, at home or abroad, with impunity.

But it comes with the price that the BB does not get to be a child very long. It is hoped you will be a model of behavior, so you don't get to screw off, or just "fuck it!" too often without disappointing your parents who are working their butts off so everyone survives and has a shot at thriving. Then there's the eternal vigilance that has to be maintained, and the law and order tactics that BB has to employ to support the "house rules". It is an honor and a total commitment post. The mantra is Responsibility First...not Wiffle Ball First. Johnny's suggestion showed me that he understood, finally, how rare this situation was for me: nothing for me to guard, to worry about, or to fix because nothing was under my control for this brief, beautiful piece of time. He didn't want me to miss it. What the hell is happening to him?

Hardball was our game through little league and high school. And we were pretty good as pitcher Johnny and catcher Jack. But we secretly dug wiffle ball, mostly because you couldn't really hurt anyone with a bad pitch you were inventing; you can literally crush the fuckin' ball if you get "good plastic" on it; and it's a trip trying to catch the crazy curves and drops of the slotted ball. The girls loved playing too, and maybe for the same reasons. Anyway, we played couples and mixed couples all afternoon. It was hours of laughing, joking, toking, drinking, and tanning. All leading to a Hibachi campfire and a good night's sleep. Tonight's rest would feature dry blankets and earplugs we fashioned from unused Marlboro filters. The raunchy smells were replaced by fresh mountain air with a hint of orange [Yukon Jack].

Around 2 am, Johnny and Caroline rumbled out the back window of the truck and escaped for short walk or something private like that. I'm sure they thought about being quiet, but Carly and I were now awake. With both of them gone, it was a good time to ask Carly if she's noticed the new attitude in JohnnyLand since the truck broke down. And now this moonlight sonata. What's happening to them?

"He's definitely been happier since we started having problems," Carly said, "I guess after you've had a lot of bad times you just need a change. Even if the change is helping with somebody else's problems, you can forget about your own." I had to agree that might be the case, "And you've seen Cabby's been happy to be around him again, now that he's into your problems and not always on her case," Carly added, "Then he responds to her smiles and her respect for him starts coming back."

"Plus the pot," I added, "I usually have to front him; now he feels like the Big Kahuna, rolling fat joints and passing 'em around. But he's always been generous when he had something. I still don't know where he got it."

All this amateur psychoanalysis was messing with our minds and our sleep time. So we decided to take a few hits and split a beer to help us catch some zzz's. Good thing it worked because Johnny had me up early, saying that Joe wanted the truck in the garage- right away. The part was here.

Skinny Al used the tire-padded front of the tow truck to push the Blue Moose into Bay #1 and then got to work welding on the new yoke. He was about done when a loud horn and booming voice brought Al to a halt and Old Joe to his feet.

"It's the Chief, Al," said Joe, looking out the office door's narrow window, "Who else would it be, startin' up a ruckus this early?"

Johnny and I watched from a safe distance as the town's chief of police entered the office, red in the face and neck; throwing his thick, hairy arms around while cursing his new, C.O.P. cruiser, color gray with red insignias. He finally slowed down and let Joe respond. I couldn't exactly hear what Joe said to him. [We had moved further away. The dude was not freak friendly]. But, if it was possible, the chief became even madder than before and stormed out after looking over to glare at the Blue Moose and Skinny Al. We could hear him peel away from the lot; so whatever the car's problem was, it wasn't poor acceleration.

Johnny immediately zipped into Joe's office to check the scene. After about 15 minutes, Johnny came out and filled me in on what had gone down: first, Joe was okay. Calm, actually. The chief is his nephew, so he doesn't take any shit from him.... or favors. Chief wanted Joe to put the cruiser in bay #1, and make it job #1 to look at the radiator. Brand new car and it's overheating. He was really fuckin' pissed. Joe had the stones to tell him we were the first job; we'd been waiting a day for the part, and we need to get home to our kids and jobs. Joe said he'd look at the cruiser right after our truck. Well, that made the top cop freak out some more. Old Joe told him to get the hell out of the garage and go to work. That's it. I thanked him for hangin' with us, but he just looked at me kinda surprised and said he don't need no

143

thanks; he always keeps his word. But the whole thing tells me I need to hide that weed better if the chief's coming back. He knows we're freaks and he'd love to bust our ass for anything, especially possession, man.

"So, tell me, how did you score that shit, Johnny? I just hafta know. Really."

"I told Mrs. Joe that I'd help her pick some more tomatoes, and cukes, and whatever else she needs.   Then I'll meet you and the ladies back at the tent...should be dried out by now. We'll have it folded before the truck's ready."

"So you're not gonna tell me, Johnny? And after I said [in falsetto] 'I love you, man.'"

"Jack, I promised not to say anything about it until after we're gone, OK?"

"I can respect that, Johnny." I suddenly felt embarrassed for asking, then recovered, "Yeah, that's good. You're gonna keep a secret, for once." I had to bust his balls a little or I'd lose my credibility with him. Still, his refusal to cop to the source was another example of his recent sense of responsibility. Could I handle it?

Johnny walked away to find a hiding place for the bowl of buds. I hoped he would be back from Mrs. Joe's garden in time to help me face the repair bill. Not that Joe would rip me off. We had seen that he was a straight guy, in the best sense, just by how he handled the chief. On the other hand, I remember him telling some college kids to screw off when they came in to buy one spark plug "to go" and not a full set of installed plugs.

"How do I make a dime selling you boys one plug that you put in yourself," he asked, "You want one plug?

Go to Zayre's. It's twenty miles that a-way."

He finally sold them one Champion plug for $3, gapped to specs. That told me he was a true businessman. He wants to make money on any job, big or small. I tried to figure what my bill would be. Joe posted the hourly labor charge--$15, but I could only guess his mark-up on parts. Then there's tax and a Sunday, after 5 p.m. tow charge. I could be looking at a total bill of $150-$200. That was a week's pay! Good thing I had a rare resource among my peers at the time: a credit card with a whopping $500 limit.

I braced Carly for what I figured Joe would charge us. She looked a little stunned, which surprised me, seeing as how she's the daughter of a radical, antique car collector who regularly spends beaucoup bread for an original radiator cap. She knew it was unavoidable, anyway, and was relieved we had the credit card.

"Does he take credit cards, Jack? Visa?" she asked.

"Whoa! I didn't think about that. I don't know. I didn't see any sign for 'We Accept' ... whatever, you know what I mean? If he doesn't, we'll have to try a postdated, personal check. Shit, I don't know. Maybe Johnny can work his magic again?

Caroline could sense we were a little worried, silently staring at nothing; so she came over to us for the lowdown. I was trying to quit smokes, but the situation called for self-indulgence. So I lit up, and the three of us took turns on the bottle of Silver Satin until we felt mellow enough to continue getting everything ready for loading and leaving.

We finished a few minutes before Al backed the truck out of the garage and drove it over to us and our pile of stuff. He said everything looked good, but he was going to take a short test drive up the mountain just to be sure there's no wobbling under load. Good idea, I thought...no need for another ride on the hook.

"Joe has the bill if you wanna look it over while I'm gone."

"Does he take credit cards, Al? Like Visa?" I wanted to know before going in there, one-on-one with Old Joe.

"Yep, he does. Visa and MasterCard with a valid I.D. that's got a picture on it."

We passed a big hurdle #1 with that news. All I needed now was Johnny to bring his mysterious goodwill with Joe and the Mrs. into the office with me. I looked around toward the garden to see if I could spot him and wave him down. No Johnny. Must be in Joe's house. What's he doin in there, learning how to make jam? I asked myself aloud.

"Johnny's in the office," said Caroline, a bit nervously, "How did he get in there?"

Carly handed me the credit card. "And here's a kiss for good luck."

"Thanks, I'll need all I can get."

Johnny was talking to Joe when I walked in the office. He didn't turn to see me, but Joe looked up at me from this seat at the desk.

"Your brother, Johnny, here, thinks I'm padding your bill," Joe grinned.

"Damn right, Joe," Johnny replied as he pushed his neck brace up with his thumb, "and I told you, right off, that I didn't want my brother ripped-off just because we were stuck here."

"What's the total, Joe?" I asked before deciding if Johnny was right or trying to bluff Joe down.

"One-hundred, twenty-five dollars and seventy-five cents."

"Does that include the tow? That's the total repair bill?"

"That's everything we did on the truck. And...I'll give you another bill for the tow, with a higher charge, so you clear the deductible. That'll get you the $25 tow back from your club membership coverage."

Johnny looked at me for my reaction. He was loyal, but he didn't really know an over-charge from a bargain. Joe handed me the itemized bill for inspection. It was a bargain. I smiled at Johnny to let him know he'd done a good job keeping the cost down.

"Johnny's a tough customer, Joe. But with letting us stay here for free, time spent getting the part, and the tow receipt, I'd say the bill is fair. I've got a Visa..." and Joe broke in.

"Who said staying here was for free? It's $30 a night." Joe said with a stern look.

When he saw my jaw drop and Johnny's face turn redder than his sunburn, Joe burst into laughter, slapping his knee and wiping tears from his eyes with an old hanky.

147

"Wish you boys could see your faces," he said after regaining his voice.

"Big joke, huh," said Johnny, "You'll be the next guy in a neck brace, old man."

Then Al started laughing while Carly and Cabby stood outside wondering what the hell was going on...only the garage guys were laughing. So they came in, hair on fire, expecting the worse. But everyone had a laugh once the joke was out.

The bill was paid, the truck packed, and the chief was back with his "hot'cruiser. It was time to go. Joe paid no mind to the chief's return, but came over with Al to say a proper 'goodbye' to his Hippie guests.

"Next time you come up, bring your wives."

"These are our wives, Joe," I protested.

"Sure they are, heh, heh, sure they are," he laughed as he winked at Carly and Caroline, who were sitting in the back, smiling back at Old Joe.

"We wouldn't settle for these guys without a ring, Joe," Carly shot back, wondering if that was at the root of Johnny and Caroline's fighting.

Suddenly, Mrs. Joe stepped in front of her large husband and thanked us for staying, and for Johnny's help with harvesting her garden. Then she handed me brown bags filled with tomatoes, cukes, green beans, and sandwiches for the ride home. I handed them over to Johnny as she gave them to me, thinking how surprisingly generous these people were to us. We thanked them again and said our last 'good byes.'

All of us wanted to stop and eat before we reached the highway home, so I asked Johnny to keep an eye out for a good place to pull over and eat those sandwiches.

"You talking about these sandwiches?" Johnny asked, as he opened the bag for me to get a good look.

The bag was full of lids packed tight with weed. There were about eight of them. I almost drove off the road.

"Mrs. Joe grows pot? She sells pot along with the carrots?"

"Mrs. Joe has cancer, Jack. She takes chemotherapy and it makes her wanna throw up. But she needs the treatments. A nurse told her marijuana can take away the nausea. But it's illegal. Then, there's the cost of buying it. So she grows it right in with the other stuff. No one out here really knows what it looks like as a full plant, so she's pretty safe doing it.

"That's sad, man. Mrs. Joe is too good to have cancer. Joe's hiding it pretty well, or maybe doesn't know," was all I could think to say, "But why is she letting you- now us- in on this; giving us all this weed?"

Johnny explained that Mrs. Joe doesn't smoke cigarettes. Nor does Joe. And she didn't know anything about rolling a joint. So she would put some in her baking. Sometimes it would be too much for her at one time; too much buzz for herself. And she had to keep Joe's cookies separate from hers. "So I guess he doesn't know about the pot, anyway."

"No offense, Johnny, but why was she telling you this?" I asked.

149

"Joe sent me up to the house for a coffee. I kind of caught her trying to roll a fatty on the porch, picking out seeds with her fingers. Well, she knew we were hippies and hippies smoke pot. So she asked me if I knew how to "take care of this stuff."

"I sure do," I said and I pulled out my papers.

Then I showed her how to clean and roll. After I brought Joe his coffee, I went back to the house and lit one up. I taught her how to inhale. It was tough at first, but she got the hang of it pretty quick. She already ingested, so a couple of good tokes and she was high. The TV was on and she just laughed at everything she watched, especially her favorite show: Lawrence Welk. Dance of the zombies is what it looked like.

I had to go. She asked me to come back early in the morning to help her harvest the lettuce. I showed the next morning, and, after working an hour, she gave me the covered, plastic bowl full of weed. Now we got all these clean lids. Good pay for an hour's work, Jack."

"Johnny," I said, "You have some bad luck and some really good luck."

"But I never know which luck to expect. So I call it pot luck."

We had a blast on the rest of the way back, and dropped our troubled couple off at their apartment, laughing again. I knew Carly and I were thinking the same thing: that Johnny and Caroline's "luck" had changed. The other changes were up to them.

La POSADA

The Newbridge Gazzette,
July 30, 1974

Mass. Tribe Sacks House of Refuge

   La Posada, a quiet, lakefront vacation chalet on
Lakeside Road, was recently occupied by a large group of
people from Massachusetts, identified as "The
Prudhomme's." This extended family of three generations
of adult males and females, with children and a number
of spouses, friends, and relatives took possession of the
"House of Refuge and Peace" under the pretense of
renting the chalet for one family for two weeks. The
chalet sleeps eight and has a sewer system designed for no
more than ten occupants. The Prudhomme party was
estimated by neighbors and bathers at the nearby beach
to number between twenty-five to thirty members, most
of whom wore Hippie attire and long hair; the men,
beards and mustaches.

   Witnesses stated that many in the group had
skinny legs and most of the adults smoked, even while in
the water. None of the tribe wore actual bathing suits on
the overcrowded beach or in the lake, but "tube tops"
were in evidence everywhere. A few of the men wore
flannel shirts over T's, dungarees, and heavy boots in the
blazing noonday sun.

   Observers in boats on the lake reported a large
number of small fish hanging from a clothesline in the
backyard of the chalet, which was also littered with
broken lounge chairs, toys, and car parts. Stone campfires
scarred the backyard grass and the boaters could smell a
strange, musky smoke when they got near the shoreline.
A freshly dug horse shoe pit, flanked by torch lights, was
spotted along the front of the deck. Further observation
ended when several young men of the tribe took to the
chalet's canoes with spear guns and hunting slingshots,

152

charged at the locals' boats and forced them to retreat to their home piers.

Other neighbors complained that La Posada's parking area was overrun, leaving vehicles parked on the narrow street and denying safe access by car to residents and visitors living further up Lakeside Road. It was also reported that fireworks could be seen shooting up from the chalet's pier and landing in the lake. No one was injured, but adjacent owners claimed they lost needed sleep standing guard with water hoses at the ready for any rockets landing on their houses or cars. Their pets were terrified by the loud display.

Fearing their secluded, upscale community was being invaded by a California -style cult, entrenched at La Posada, a group of neighbors contacted the owner of the chalet, Mr. Harold Shelton of Leominster, Mass., who promised to call his tenant immediately and visit his chalet, if necessary, "this weekend." Neighbors were not calmed by Mr. Shelton's promise and filed a complaint with local police. Thus far, Newbridge authorities have "no comment" on whether any formal investigation into those complaints is in progress.

The article above was cut out of the paper and taped to a dozen or more frig doors. They stayed there long after the summer vacation my parents spent with us kids at the lake, ended. From the neighbors' end of the microscope, I suppose the article was close to being factually correct and their fears not without cause. On the other hand, even the article's author and the police thought the locals were guilty of losing their cool and being un-neighborly. In truth, a case could be made that our "tribe" was harassed and our privacy violated by the neighbors' blatant spying activities, perhaps motivated by classism and anti-Hippie prejudice in the well-to-do community of out-of-state, summer residents.

Local Mainers couldn't have given a shit—they looked like we did, without the beads and bumper stickers [Impeach Nixon]. It was the summer of '74, and the battle lines had been drawn long ago between our turned on, burn this, free that, stop- the- war, legalize what's in my boot movement, and the Establishment's "love it or leave it" crowd. Our tribes were destined to clash at the normally homogenous, socially insulated enclave. We had invaded their refuge from the world's problems, especially the drug-crazed peacenik masses yearning to make America live up to its billing as the "land of the free."

The poor owner got stuck in the middle. He agreed to rent his chalet to my calm, soft-spoken father over the telephone. My dad's description of his sons and daughters, the grandchildren—two in wheelchairs-- and how much he loved and respected the peace and quiet of fishing on a Maine lake, instantly won Mr. Shelton's trust. The only specific number regarding the chalet that was mentioned was the high rental cost, which my union welder father could easily cover [especially for such a large group, he silently thought]. Mr. Shelton didn't know my father possessed a Zen tranquility gene that helped him survive the noise and conflicts of eight kids, six growing into their teens together, in a three bedroom house, sharing one bath. By the time they guided us into our "tweens," Mom and Dad's chaos tolerance threshold was way high, and they did it without booze or drugs...just love, and an OFF switch in their heads for sweating the small stuff. It was this special set of parents and their family that Mr. Shelton actually allowed into his pristine posada, along with the brood's spouses, lovers and friends. Some relatives visited, too. So, just like the rappers and sports analysts bark: Let's break it down.

I am the oldest of four brothers. Three of us were

born less than a year apart. The fourth brother was born three sisters and seven years after me. Besides having parents in common, the brothers all share something else: we are white men who strongly resemble a different, well-known, black man.

I've been called a white Sammy Davis Jr. by drunks and sober people, alike. I not only look like Sammy, but also over- laugh like him, joke and dance like him, and drink like Dean Martin, too, like him. We're very talky, overly conscious of our clothes, grooming, and height. We look best with a moustache and dressed for a party or event. We have an instant rapport with other "cool guys" regardless of their specific "look," race, or religion. Sammy's hair was wavy on top, combed back tight on the sides to meet in a "duck's ass" pattern in the back. This is still my basic style, although now in grey tones, for accent. Despite many defects, my "Yes, I Can" attitude has won me some success... and the love of my life. On the down-side, like Sammy, I have also been threatened by mafia for being with the "wrong woman." An accident left Sammy with only one good eye, whereas I have two bad eyes, which makes us even. We could both see well enough.

Brother Johnny is Richard Pryor in looks and facial expressions, especially that "scared shitless" face Pryor puts on, and his quick, jumpy over-reactions. He loves to entertain. He doesn't tell jokes, he acts them. He is comedy in motion. Like Pryor, Johnny gets into trouble easily, and has had, and been responsible for, numerous accidents, the worst involving flames. He also has real talent [the piano] that somehow makes him want to live dangerously. Pryor and Johnny aren't the only men who prefer blondes. But it's an unstated requirement for Johnny, though he will dally with all women. Some have provided a fair share of the danger he always sought out of any situation at work or play. Now termed an

155

"adrenalin rush" addiction, these guys personify the sad clown when not pursuing danger.

Bobby is usually quiet. He moves at a confidently slow pace. He surprises new comers with his incisive wit and dry sense of humor, gained by keenly observing the quirks of surviving in a large family. Bobby is physically strong and can be threatening in a good humored way. He is Bill Cosby, and born without any cartilage in his nose for extra facial similarity to Bill. He loves slippers, and PJ's, and crazy sweaters, just like Cosby wore on his show. He often gets off by laughing at himself. Other times, he is very serious. It's best to get to recognize which mode he's in. A "one woman" man, as Bill was thought to be, many women find these two irresistible because of their laid-back mojo.

Anyone remember "DYNOMITE!!!" Jimmy Walker? That's bro Teddy: Tallish, slim, hawk-nosed, and even a nice head of curly blond Afro. Has quick intelligence, but not sure what to use it for. So he chases after different things. And though he is a good man, those things are often not good. He and JJ are also good ears when you need to talk, and good eyes for spotting hot chicks. These guys just don't have much luck attracting and keeping them. Both bros are tougher than they look, but are still very sensitive to others' pain. When JJ left the show 'cuz he was having trouble with drugs, Teddy, in make-up, could've filled in and played JJ. But he was also having trouble with drugs.

Ironically, though we resemble these famous entertainers who are quite distinct in the public eye, my brothers and I appear very similar in public, even among people who see us often and have known us through a few life-stages. I've been attacked from behind at a deli counter by a local derelict that knew all the brothers, but wrongly thought I was Johnny until I flipped him around

156

so he could see my face better. Our wives and girlfriends were often embarrassed by grabbing the wrong ass. But despite the closeness of our physical appearance, the brothers go their own way; rarely seek each other for advice, never plan any "brother" events, and have no agreed upon agenda on anything consequential or trivial. We only band together to fight an outside threat, partner in horseshoes, or play on a softball team, a.k.a. Beer Team.

My sisters, on the contrary, all look very different from each other: a curly copper-haired one; a taller, brown haired one; a curly blond, round faced one, and a blond straight haired one. They are all attractive and fun to have around. They love a good time, and can joke and party at the same level of any guy they chose. They learned well from their own mother how to mother their children, especially the handling of explosive materials. After that, it's all pretty much "Vivre la difference." One sister has the drive and ability to command of a field general; a loving but fiercely protective force. Another sister is shy, sweet and a faithful believer who cannot be moved. Another is a caring, loved and respected health care professional. She is a master of detached and rational control in a medical crisis and has faced tragic loss with amazing strength. Another sister has the talented eyes, hands, and focus of a fragile, reclusive artist. But she is mild tempered, sociable, and emotionally tough. All my sisters shine in a different way.

Their voices are distinct, especially the one who's tone deaf. Their figures are just as distinct, but they're all very attractive. I'd get into more details, but don't want to get hurt! No one has ever mistaken any of my sisters for another. So, those of us who know them best are amazed how they often they act as one entity, a masterfully integrated team of people with varied abilities. They somehow come to agree on a goal, devise a schedule of

157

action, create the preceding propaganda campaign, complete the mission and assessment of results—everything—without a recognizable meeting. Somehow, they do not leave behind any evidence of how it was done.

Naturally, we became curious about the earthly creators of our diverse, four boys/ four girls, sibling cell. How did they get hooked up? And why the surge of pregnancies, the high number, even for post WWII couples? Did they want to energize a genetic variety pack, or just keep trying to get that perfect baby for the camera? Was it love, or was it just sex? The more we looked for insight from the factual data, the more we realized how little our parents told us about their lives before we took over their lives. Our skilled interrogator, whom we will not name, couldn't get much out of them after years of trying every angle and peeking through every crack in the wall. But when we finally pooled our bits and pieces of intel for their thirtieth anniversary, a small fact book began to take shape about our 'loco parenti.'

Dad was a quiet, young musician, recently released from soldiering with the U.S. Army-Air Force in the CBI, China-Burma-India Theatre of World War Two. Ma was a young, beautiful, Nun-to-Be, recently graduated from the College of Our Lady of Notre Dame, Baltimore, Md. There were no dating services then, no Confidential section of the local paper, nor any Internet sites to meet other people. So they met by physically going to a popular dance hall of their generation called Rhodes-on-the-Pawtuxet, in Cranston, Rhode Island, their native state... and hoped for the best.

We never asked, and they never told, the exact mechanism that put them in each other's arms on a particular evening [too icky for parent/child discussion in our family]. Maybe it was a common friend who introduced them or a glance across a crowded ballroom, but the quiet musician soon broke up with his pre-war girlfriend and the Nun-to- Be declined to take her Final Vows of obedience, poverty, and chastity. They must have dated, but again, we have no direct evidence or testimony. We do know that in August of 1947, Fast Eddy married Sister Betty in a big Church wedding and they produced eight children in ten years. This assertion is supported by original, untouched photographs. They proved that if you kiss chastity goodbye, but remain obedient to the Church's birth control methods, you can become poverty stricken from parenthood.

They lived happily, thinking themselves rich with children. They worked at good jobs and made enough money for other, smaller families to be considered "rich." So we were never poor. Likewise, my dad was, in fact, not fast, but so very deliberate in doing everything that it drove Sister Betty nuts. For her part, Sister Betty soon lost all support for "obedience" and found some comfort in teaching her children to "question authority" long before war protesters printed the phrase on a bumper sticker. She challenged everything supported by the "Establishment," but accepted responsibility to help needy people and social causes without hesitation. Once a patient novitiate, she became a person who would literally knock walls down with a sledge hammer if she wanted a larger dining room and Fast Eddie was slow in getting to it. He'd come home from a ten-hour day and "Voila!" He missed the "groundbreaking ceremony" but would soon start a slow-but-sure, well-constructed remodeling of three rooms.

We did need the open floor plan because each of us kids had at least one "bring-home" friend every couple of evenings, meaning there would be, counting Gramma, at least 11, maybe 20 people in the house, plus an

159

unknown number of yard and porch people. Our parents were now Steady Eddie and Poor Betty.

They had so many kids that they couldn't socialize with any adults, including most of their relatives, because their family didn't travel well and would fill anyone's house to over-capacity if they did manage to visit. Having people over was an easier fit in their large Victorian, but there was no privacy for adults in their home's layout and room assignment. If they went out by themselves disaster would strike whether the older kids babysat or an outsider took the job. Outside sitters couldn't be found, anyway, if they were told the ugly facts of their workload. Ed and Betty knew adults where they worked and the oil man, the guys at the gas station, and the Avon lady. Neighbors were absent or hostile, but 'sonofa bitch, their kids came over.

So my parents became adjusted to a life lived almost entirely with their brood. That life included the summer vacation, a crazy attempt to get away from it all and find some recreation, relax a bit while the children were out of school for three hot months. They also needed to create a diversion for the kids to distract them from burning the house down. But if we couldn't all fit in an eight room house, how many beach shanties would we need? Who would rent to our demographic in the first place? No one. So we would split up vacations with each parent's family, girls going to one place in July; the boys going to another in August.

As we got older and more socialized, it became possible for everyone to go camping together at these places called campgrounds. We had only tented in our own yard or the natural woods. Campgrounds had electrical and water hook-ups; community lavatories and showers, just like school. The better ones had a pond or river front for swimming and fishing, even a store and gift shop. But these amenities soon wore thin, and New England weather is consistently inconsistent. You could return home with arthritis or frostbite, sun stroke or dehydration, fly bites to keep you scratching all of fall and winter.

Our parents had arrived at that age where they required comfortable lodging with the outdoor experience. La Posada was the perfect place, if not a perfect fit. It would not guilt me to weasel my way into getting the place first, answering questions later. But my father would never lie to a man who was renting out his summer lodging. Still, the truth was he could never be sure how many of us would actually show up on "trip day" and how many others we would bring with us. There could be five—there could be twenty-five. Without a dependable number, why should he miss an opportunity to return to the area of his honeymoon with the ripened fruit of his parenthood?

Besides, his kids weren't wild Vandals anymore. They were now a mix of skilled tradesmen, artists, supervisors, college graduates, Navy veterans, a book keeper, an office manager, and a nurse. All he saw were the positives, and there were many. He figured that in the end, it would all work out.

Or if everybody came, bringing too many ideas, opinions, and full bladders, it wouldn't work out quite so well. My parents could depend on the women to help carry out Mother's well proven plan for fun without fatalities. They would provide meals, children with proper attire and medications, sun blocks, a workable sleeping arrangement that did not break any taboos, and planned entertainment.

The men would pack the stuff up and somehow make it fit in their vehicle, including in-transit entertainment. But their real bag was providing alcoholic beverages, and mixers, Slim-Jims, bromides, sporting gear, smoking gear, live bait, bug blocks, fireworks, music, and spontaneous illegal/dangerous activities for themselves and the kids. When they realized the lake was stocked and reasonably clean, they would add "fishing for food" to their mission statement. This division of labor was time proven to foster enduring memories of hilarity, fine meals with all your loved ones, accomplishing new things and revisiting favorite things. But this open invitation to vacation "our way" at a serene and well cared for place, protected from the usual discomforts, might be pushing our luck, the positive limits of our collective karma, and the sanitation codes of Newbridge, Maine.

I wasn't told about the septic limitations, and for good reason. I am a pessimistic person, and hyper critical of everything I am exposed to-- even if I love the person, place, or thing. I have to analyze before I can approve. Plans don't have to be perfect, but I need to know what the imperfections are. It took me about twenty of my, then, twenty-six years to perfect this outlook. There was plenty of anecdotal and hard core documentation from past outings to support my low expectations for this Prudhomme Rendezvous. This is probably why no one told me about it. I'd only point out any flaws in the plan and the circumstances set against it. When we were younger, the vacation incidents were minor slip-ups, like leaving Newport Beach on a hot day without 4 year old Teddy, or Johnny getting stuck on top of Frog Rock in the woods of Connecticut. Now we were larger, stronger, long-haired freaks who had experienced sex and drugs and could do serious damage to the gingerbread world and ourselves. But the family had factored in the "wet blanket" effect of my advice, made adjustments, and put the plans in concrete before asking me anything but secondary questions like, "If you had to choose, would you rather sleep with one of your brothers or a brother-in-law?"

I had no choice but to go, and that gave me a lighter feeling than if I had more responsibility for green lighting this trip. My next strategy for avoiding a bummer with the group decision was a sweet n'sour sauce of positive visualizations and lowered expectations. But even I couldn't lower my expectations enough to shrug off the scene that Carly, brother Teddy, and I walked into on our arrival, the second day of the communal vacation.

We were a day behind the main body of vacationers because I had to fix the muffler on my '69 Pontiac LeMans before we left. I made a quick job of it and paid the consequences later as we drove five hours with a loose tailpipe pointing up at the rear bumper, instead of down and away from the car. But we made it to La Posada. That was good bad news-- we didn't blow up. But some things in the trunk were melted or hot, including our case of once cold beer. The rear tail light was transformed into a twisted, plastic patty-melt, overflowing to fuse with the wrap-around bumper.

We wanted time to grieve our spoiled stuff, but we were interrupted by shouts and crying coming from the back of the chalet. They sounded like they belonged to the last person we'd expect to be raising a racket--my mother.

We could hear my father's laughs mixed in there, too. Scurrying down the outside stairs to the lakeside deck, we halted at the sight of my father trying to gently pin my mother against the sliding door. I walked toward them, becoming informed as I moved along that my non-drinking mom flipped out after downing one gin tonic. My father was sober, but losing control laughing at how 'gonzo his normally stoic wife was. The result was a scuffle, as he tried to console and restrain her at the same

163

time. The action was going on in front of the door, so that some people were trapped in the kitchen, shouting their advice through the screens while those out on the deck were noisily corralling the royal pair, in an effort to quiet things down. Watching my father slide step left and right, my mother charge forward, then stop fall back and crumple in laughter was enough evidence to prove that Central Command was radically "on vacation..." something my low expectations never expected.

This caused some nervous laughter and a bit of shock among the core family. We were not prepared for this. Neither were the neighbors, who were already treated, the night before, to a loud, drunken lawn chair duel between two of our brother-in-laws who are also brothers. Once all the outdoor furniture was broken, they continued to hammer each other in the lake, which gave the sounds of their fists hitting flesh and mangled swearing that special echo effect that "kicks in" over the water under a mountain. It was typical alcohol-related behavior in both cases. We potheads wouldn't be quick to fighting after turning-on, or erratic emotional behavior after one toke. Paranoid behavior could occur—sometimes. But not until after years of getting wasted, or some good reason-- like the neighbors getting busted for holding one lid.

Most of the time, these sturdy lads drank and laughed—period. My mother wouldn't drink and Dad wouldn't have to keep her from running into the lake. Our ring family of in-laws, partners, and relatives were dependable and capable of keeping us from bumming out over one incident in fifty years. They could be a little objective about a sudden, emotional roller coaster ride—happens all the time. But the core family of brothers and sisters had nowhere to hang this behavior. We had only seen other parents display it at weddings and American Legion dances.

164

Things calmed down and we eventually got to exchange stories about our trip up there with their stories and discoveries about the chalet and the lake. Our close cousin, Joni, and my oldest sister tried to move our attention and brighten our mood by announcing the dinner entrée. It was just what I was afraid of: the couple dozen undersized fish, I saw pinned on the clothesline in the warm sun.

Everybody was so psyched for this minnow fry, waiting all day for it to be cleaned, and cooked up on the campfires for tonight's dinner. I just wanted to puke looking at it all. I was known as a good cook, so my disapproval was heavy. At the risk of being called "Fussy Jack" [again], I simply said that I wouldn't eat any—there would be more for them, and they would need it to feel a meal in their gut.

"Just try it," Carly pleaded, "You like fish."

"I do. But those things are just pieces of skin with bones inside."

Wayne came over to help persuade me. Wayne: the Nordic hunter, the body builder, swimmer, and scholar, sister's paramour, sports car racer, tree chopper, and Scotch drinker. He was the real deal-- honest, fearless, handsome, optimistic, generous, funny, and greatest friend to all my brothers and me.

"Ya gotta try the fish, Jack. We all caught some of them, even baby Joey. It's a tribute to the fisherman to eat some. Come on, man. They thought you'd be impressed."

"I've told you before, man. Fresh water fish tastes like the water it came out of—stagnant algae, with ten bones in every bite. No fuckin' way. They're mostly kivers and sunfish, anyway. You know what they're good for--- catching a bigger fish that you can actually eat... like a bass."

"There's bass out there--humongous ones. I could see them just three feet below the boat, the water is that clear. But they're not going for our bait. Mark, Ritchie, Joey and I dove in, and the bass stayed right there. Then he started moving slowly, leading us around to keep us on him and away from the nest. I swam just above the weeds he kept leading us into, but Mark—he glided right through them! The water was so clear I could see the waving, bright green, lake grass contrasting with his alabaster body and reddish hair, and then covering him every few seconds, as he moved with the current like he was becoming a part of some underwater world," Wayne enthusiastically shared.

Then he offered more details of the action, and a plan... "But even if we caught up with the bass, we had nothing with us that could capture him. Forget grabbing him with your hands. Mark had a hand on its tail, Ritchie grabbed the body and it just slipped right out and sped up...it's their world down there. So tomorrow, I'm going to see if I can get a frog spear or something like a trident and we're gonna snorkel down and spear a big one," Wayne promised.

"That sounds honest—no attempt to trick the fish, just go directly into the water and spear it like a wild boar. Hunting underwater, a Mike Nelson-Sea Hunt kind of thing, but doesn't even that require a license? Does anyone here have a fishing license of any kind for Maine? Any state?"

"I think fishing rights come with the chalet. Besides, who's gonna see what we're doin' underwater?"

166

"The surrounding neighbors will figure it out, or other fishermen. Johnny says we're being watched all the time by the neighbors. Is he just stoned paranoid or what, bud?"

"I don't know, really. Mark, Ritchie and I are out on the lake all day. Lulu and the girls always go to the beach, which they say is kinda crowded with straights telling 'em to read the swimming rules. They just give them the finger. Don't worry about it Bosco [alternate name], you've had a long ride and it's time for a beer. Tomorrow we'll have to take that muffler system down and lay it out right over here under the porch spotlight, in case it becomes night work. We'll clamp it loosely, make sure it's long enough to clear the bumper and then put it in. This time, let's remember to tighten everything."

"Pointing the right way, too? Yeah, I'll do that after getting a tan on the little catamaran over there. Have you tried it yet?" I asked about the small double hull sailboat tied to the La Posada pier.

"No, we've been using the rowboat and the canoe to fish. You and Carly oughta' take it out tomorrow. I think there's enough room on the canvass deck to play captain and cabin boy—or girl. Hey! Don't look at me like that. I'm making a good suggestion. You think you're gonna' be able to let the "stallion" loose up in the loft with two other couples and six kids surrounding you? Take advantage of the privacy of the lake. Just switch who's on top every few minutes so no one gets a sunburned ass."

"If the loft is for the couples with kids, where are you and Lou sleeping at the 'peaceful refuge'...in the MG?"

167

"No way, Jose. Johnny and Caroline probably would. You know, like last summer when they camped in the Great Swamp, sleeping in little Rodney's Indian teepee; their legs sticking out into the rain. No car cramps for us, Jack. No leaky roof over our heads. We're with the "couples without kids" on the screened porch, in fresh sleeping bags and home-made quilts, right above the horseshoe pit."

"There's no horse shoe pit over there."

"It's on the list for tomorrow," Wayne said as he pulled an index card from his back pocket and unfolded it, reading his list aloud, "We're going into the village for: beer, wine, ice, frog spears, postcards, popcorn, candy bars, marshmallows, and Tiki candles—if they have any— for night-time horse shoes."

"Sounds like a full day for the little people under the mountain, Wayne. I'm going to the frig to find myself some food I can eat, even if it's Susie's meatballs--cold-- from the big pot."

"Then don't forget to bring water and some plop-plop, fizz-fizz to the loft at bedtime, my friend. It would be a heavy trip in the dark, stepping over sleeping bodies, stoned, your chest burning, searching for some acid relief."

"I can dig it. That's why Carly has some foil packets in her pocketbook and water in the bedside mini-cooler. At this point in my drinking career, sleeping can be dangerous. The enemy is not the meatballs acting alone. It's the beer and beef jerky, smoking weed, popcorn, shots of scotch, and the meatballs brewing together that send the burning gases up my throat. It's like my stomach is a car battery being charged with the caps off."

"So, now you're the human battery. What happened to 'the white Sammy Davis, Jr.'? Is that a three-year or five-year warranty you're carrying around? Maybe we could get some jumper cables on your nuts to start the MGA this winter."

"Maybe you should be careful Joey doesn't put a frog spear up your butt by accident, thinking you were a large mouth bass."

"Take it easy, Sammy," Wayne laughed, "You're the guy who thinks his little beer belly is a battery."

And the laughs flowed, as the sun set and the mosquitoes came out starving for blood. It was time to take advantage of the La Posada the refuge...this time from insect attack. Once we were all in for the night, it became obvious our clan literally filled the chalet to the rafters. Squeezing from room to room was a hassle. If somebody went into the dining room, filled for a card game, only their luck could run out. They were stuck in there. Likewise, if we'd get thirsty hanging around the screened porch, it meant having to yell into the kitchen for someone to send a beer over to ya' via human chain. Usually it would be warm by the time it reached its destination...or nearly empty. The loft was filled with kids and responsible people watching them. The lines for the single toilet started wherever you were—just stand up {except in the loft}, look toward the bathroom door, and inch along until you merged with the other lines. Checking out the panorama, I decided it was time for a body count; so Carly performed a sight estimate of the assemblage—twenty-five souls hiding from the mosquitoes.

Getting up and ready the next day had to be done one family at a time, drawn by lot. Wayne, Lulu, and cousin Mark put on a three hour, continuous breakfast-- a base line playing below the cacophony of the bathroom key changes. And since private dressing had to rotate as well, the whole process required the orchestration of all the movements into a completed work. As each family unit rolled off the assembly line, they normally set about their preparations for their own activities. The pier, boats, and the beach, were all right there at the lake frontage. But today everyone wanted to go to the same place—the village to shop. Apparently, Wayne's list was not the only one.

The family initially arrived at La Posada in seven cars, but not more than two at a time. All seven driving into the village would be hard to overlook. Not that we wanted to steal into town—we were quite used to attracting the stares, glares and dropped jaws of the host population wherever we went together, especially with the wheelchairs. But here in the backwoods, we would surely paint the picture of the Hippie Caravan, flooding into town to "sell drugs to kids" and "seduce the young men and women" with our sexually explicit clothing, or lack thereof. Eyes would follow us in every store we entered, watching for shoplifting and breakage. Some would alert the cops to watch for drinking alcohol in open containers, and public urination. That would be a big cloud over our heads while we were just trying to mellow out in nature and enjoy the quaint village's friendly ambience. Fortunately, Central Command was back on duty. Mom and Dad had a solution that would discourage some of us, but avoid the "invader" status that surely awaited all if we came en masse.

Their plan was to take just one beaucoup roomy car: Dad's '72 Chrysler New Yorker, a.k.a., The Living Room on Wheels. Six adults could ride inside, with a trunk large enough for two dead "good fellas" and shovels. That's why the model is designated a "New Yorker". But it was more aptly a "Brooklyn". Or fill it

170

with lots of food, groceries, fishing rods, bait, Tiki candles, frog spears and the rest of Wayne's list—and it's the Chrysler "Mainer." By any name, it was as close to a limo, without being one, as any vehicle on the road. It looked new. It was luxurious. It was important to my parents to make a good impression on the villagers after the poor start with the "lakers." In the end, the village was crawling with obnoxious day- tourists, who sufficiently offended the locals that we made quick friends with the store owners, license sellers, and police force—who were impressed with Johnny's joke "arrest" of Caroline for trying to buy liquor while being a minor; flashing his toy badge and ordering her to "spread 'em against the wall, patting her down, and putting her in plastic handcuffs. His show was so true-to-television that they didn't bust him for impersonating a police officer; a felony in states without a sense of humor.

Wayne, and his sea hunting pack, scored three frog spears to try as underwater weapons against the wily small mouth bass in the lake. There is supposed to be a certain strain of these bass that will not be caught on a line, whatever the bait or lure...ever. This type may be what he saw under his canoe, staring back at him and his fishing pole. If so, Mr. Sea Hunt had the right idea in going after them, underwater. But I didn't how he planned to hit them without a proper spear gun. What fish, smart enough to suspect bait, would pose for someone while they slowly lunged at them with a hand held spear? Wayne would find out.

Returning to La Posada, the delegated shoppers rejoined the rest of the group, except Ma and Pa who had a message waiting for them from the owner. They went into their bedroom to make their return call away from the laughing, crying, beer can popping din of the kitchen. A short time later, they called Suzanne and me in for an old fashioned meeting of the elders. It was the first time I

171

visited their room. It was a knotty pine refuge within the "place of refuge," featuring a vaulted ceiling [a modern touch at the time] and a fireplace insert with glass doors. No moose head on the wall, but otherwise, perfectly chosen furnishings completed the room's warm, nouveau rustique glow. Maybe it was the pot thinking, but I suddenly realized my parents were over fifty and never in their lives had they laid their heads down in any place as quiet and comforting as this room. I remember thinking how tough re-entry to their real world would be if they stayed here and relaxed by themselves. Their faces gave me the feeling that they were about to fall back to Earth sooner than planned.

"We, ah, had a call...from, ah, the owner—Mr. Shelto. No, ah, what's his..." my father began in the way he does when he's pondering the whole scene and the details become forgettable.

"Shelton, Ed. Mr. Shelton called from his house. Some of the neighbors called and..."

"Lemme finish what I 'm saying, Betty. Will ya'?" Dad cut back in, wanting to use his low-voiced, calm tone so that we didn't freak out. "One of the neighbors, he didn't say which one, called to tell him there were fifteen of us staying here."

Susie and I couldn't stifle a laugh. Did someone say fifteen, or fifty? Fifteen? That was a wicked, low-ball estimate, or they must believe we're all in one place at the same time. The reality was that ten to fifteen of us were in three places at any given time. Lucky break, we thought. Not lucky enough, Dad explained. And for the first time, I was informed of the sewage limitation: ten carbon-based life forms inhabiting the chalet at any time. Suzanne and I knew that if my parents owned the chalet, we'd immediately put in another septic system...maybe

172

that day, twice as large, and exceed the minimum capacity. But Ma and Pa didn't own it, and the lake was right there to receive the overflow that would bubble up some time soon. Pollution of the lake would be a crime, but the sour odor of toilet water nosing out the minty fragrance of fresh pines and sweet, wild honeysuckle would be a sin. No one wanted that.

Orders would be given to pee in the woods, wash in the lake, and stop shaving. But the owner wasn't taking any chances that we could stretch the system. He said he'd be coming up in three days to be sure we were down to ten people, maximum, or we'd all have to leave and my parents would forfeit their prepaid second week.

"Your mother and I want to go back home and bring back the tent trailer. Seven people could sleep in it and use its bath and shower. That would ease the overcrowding right here and now. Later on, seven or more of us could drive it away to a nearby tenting park whenever we had to make the family instantly "smaller." The problem is getting it here before the owner shows up. Can you two keep things under control tomorrow while we're gone?"

Of course we could. Only did it all our lives. Besides, the whole idea of going civilized at a dude place like this was to make the vacation easier for them. We could still hack the leaky tent scene: cooking everything over a fire pit, no showers, sleeping on tree roots --the "back to nature" trip. And we could have split for the trailer, saving them the ride. The conveniences of the chalet were for them to enjoy. But Paps wouldn't let us drive the trailer. At least we got them to hang loose for a day and just kick back before leaving. The owner's visit was going to be cool now that we had a solution. And the weather forecast for the next day was out of sight: low 80's, clear all day, a slight breeze – the kind of day that

173

keeps people living in Ningland— a day too rare to spend driving in a car or a living room on wheels.

The news about the specific nature of our problem was not what we were expecting, but how the owner became hip to it was no surprise at all. The word from Ed and Betty was to keep the young muscles' minds on fishing and horse shoe pits and away from ideas of neighborly payback. The women were righteously pissed at the wagging tongues, but had more devious retaliation in mind than tipping over some canoes and undetectable, car engine damage. Whatever forms the response would take, they were put on hold. We had a lake to enjoy together and preparations for a totally mellow sun day.

The fishing parties headed out, with real anglers, such as Johnny and Teddy taking rods and reels in canoes; the spear fishers, Ritchie, Mark, and our own "man in the wilderness," Wayne, taking the boat with Carly as official photographer and lookout. The rest of the clan went for the sunny beach [and possible OK Corral] or stayed at the chalet. I was in the latter group as the designated kid sitter, watching them fish and play on our pier. Actually, they just ran, or wheeled, around from the pier through the water to the lawn and back again, creating a mud beach. They never did any one thing for more than three minutes except make happy noise. The exceptions were Rachael and little Bobby, who spent hours training snails to move in parade formation. Being in charge of all this while stoned and sucking down beers is not easy. At day's end, I complained bitterly about it to all the people who left me behind.

"Why didn't you at least get a tan?" some chided me for copping an attitude that bringing down their "perfect day" buzz.

"Because it's not safe to close your eyes and sit still

174

while seven kids swing hooks around your face. That's why. Did I forget to mention the near drownings and worm eating contests I had to snuff out?" Only a fool would have expected gratitude from this tanned, fun crowd. I must have forgotten the advice of Johnny Hulk: never expect the positive, but always prepare for the negative. Right on, man.

There was a general sense that I was pissed. A change of topic was required, and Johnny had it. "How'd the spear fishing go, Captain Nimrod? The bass kick your ass?" he busted Wayne.

"Are you kiddin', Stick? It was intense. It started yesterday when we were in the boat, getting no hits, and there—right below us in the clear water—was a small mouth bass guarding its nest...about six pounds. That's why we bought the frog spears: so that, today, we could swim up to the nest, surround this fish before he could escape into the current, and nail him with a spear.

I had one corner of the triangle, Ritchie on my right and Mark on my left. We slowly moved in together, closing the bass into a smaller and smaller area. All this time, the fish stayed still with its tail in my direction, its eyes on Ritchie and Mark. So, it figured that I would go for it from the blind side. Seemed like an easy hit, but when you're underwater with a fish that size, it's more intimidating than a fifty pound fish out of the water on a pier, gasping for breath. Anyway, I'm just about to lunge at the bass when it turned on a dime, facing me so that it was instantly a slim target with eyes fixed on me, like I was the prey. Holy shit! That's when Ritchie went for its side. Fuckin' thing shot up and out of the water at a 45 degree angle so fast that Ritchie looked like he was going to spear Mark, who was right across from him. Mark was still starting at the spot where the fish used to be, so he didn't see Ritchie's spear coming at him until the last second. It all looked like slow motion... except the fish. It was heavy, right Mark?"

But Mark didn't jump in quite fast enough with eye-witness support. Johnny quickly went back to his ribbing.

"So Mr. Suits" [addressing Wayne by his surname], Johnny intoned like a prosecuting attorney, "What you're saying is that you have no fish for dinner. Ritchie almost speared Mark, following your plan to stab a fish. Finally, you shit your trunks when this huge, six-pound fish eye-balled you in the middle of your attack [slight pause]. You're no fisherman, Suits." Johnny concluded, pointing a finger at the accused hero, summarizing his case for the jury of stunned, stoned, freaks in the kitchen.

"Guilty," Wayne replied in his usual good-natured way, "But, hey, I caught a great memory. And I've got cold Heinekens left, and some tequila and a bag o' fried pork rinds to soothe my wounds. What did you catch, Johnny? Poison Ivy?" and he began to choke on some half-swallowed pork rinds, laughing at his own retort.

The answer for dinner was then clearly decided: The Pizza Barn, which was exactly that...no cultural motifs, no private tables, nothing else on the menu except drinks by-the-pitcher. The high ratio of banged up, muddy, old pick-up trucks to cars announced that it was a local hangout. Fortunately, our party was welcomed for our "non-tourist" look. To the working owner and waitress, we also looked like a big tab and tip for a Tuesday night. If not, then a damned good fight for a Tuesday night. The barn's sound system was playing some good tunes that we all agreed on; the taste of the pizza surprised; and we tipped like Rhode Islanders after getting their tax refund check. A-Yeh.

We left with everybody we brought, and returned to the chalet for fireworks, courtesy of Young Eddie's Sky Writers. We always wondered where Eddie got his fireworks, illegal in most Eastern states. But even in an era before "Don't ask...don't tell" we knew better than to press him on it and he never told. It was better that way if the cops caught us lighting them. Eddie wisely chose the chalet's fishing pier, which was easily closed off to curious children, away from the trees, and surrounded by water. Artistically speaking, the pier offered an ideal launching point to create a widespread bursting of colors reflected off the rippled water, expanding the sky and silhouetting the trees against the shifting backdrop of the still mountain. With each explosion, we released a screamed exhale at the brilliant geometry of each scattered burst, and then silently absorbed the sonic "poom!" to our chests that soon followed. For some reason, the closest neighbors came out to water their lawns in the dark. Joey said they were probably dodging a watering ban. It was odd that their dogs weren't barking, as they usually do. Maybe we just couldn't hear them.

All this release was arousing a latent, but well tuned, vibrant energy among many of the spectators. Only the onset of sleepiness in the children and coolness in the air kept the couples from slinking off into the woods next to the pier for some coupling action. The mosquitoes were the deciding factor for those without kids. Everyone had to behave while the carbon dioxide-sensitive blood suckers were on patrol. Two citronella Tiki candles could not cut it in this country. We had to bury our carnal desires in sleep. But I was truly grateful just to sleep next to my wife, and not forced into a Spartan sleeping arrangement that might result in some drunken, hairy, honk-nosed dude jabbing at my ass in the middle of the dark night, thinking I was his wife who hadn't shaved her legs.

The sex-less night was followed by the flawless day. Sunny skies and warm, dry air on the same day are unfairly rare in Ningland. Even lovers and children understand this. So the parents didn't have to push their kids to get ready. Singles jumped their morning spooning session to buy more sun time. Each part of each family got it together for the particular action that looked like fun and went for it. I didn't think about how this selection process evolved, I just grew up with it. Dragooning loved ones into a variety of activities required no bulletin boards, or sign-up sheets, drawing straws, or assigning captains to form teams. There was no time for all that structure. The vacationers just melded with the group heading toward something they felt like doing. Somehow, the people numbers came to fit the size of the beach, or the raft, or the number of life jackets. Only Wayne and my son, Rod, had even been to a bona fide summer camp. Neither of them could get down with his institutionalized nature experience. Wayne ate soap at night 'till he got sick and they sent him home. Rod ate only grated cheese until the severity of his constipation demanded immediate parental rescue.

"What are you planning on doin', Jack?" Robby asked as though he was having a hard time choosing between a couple of things himself. And that was how it usually was—one thing would be something to do with the immediate family; the other, just something out of the ordinary with other guys or something really radical, suspicious, and guilt inspiring--doing something by yourself.

I had one pursuit in mind that I was kind of hung up on: an on-board picnic with Carly that Wayne had suggested. After last night, the idea of getting away with her on the catamaran-- a little lunch, a fat joint, creating a sensuous wake while gliding along the lake-- would make an excellent diversion from the herd of kids, the

178

bony fish, and the stressed out toilet. We might even forget about Watergate for a while.

"I want to take that 'cat' far, far out on the lake with Carly, Bobby. Get a tan, get stoned and make her moan. No particular order, just all happening at once." I replied. Bobby gave a quick, low laugh at my deliberately annoying rhymes. That made it clear he knew I was trying to make him laugh, and he was laughing... at me.

"You're 'far out', alright, but think of this: the farther you are from here, the closer you are to there." Bobby went along with the put-on.

"That's heavy, brother. Are you sure someone isn't sprinkling hash over your Cheerios? You have a point; I could drift away, but closer. I dig it, man. I'll have to look for the right spot to drop anchor."

To make this idea happen, I had to find a dependable and fun volunteer to take our kids with them. Usually someone would be glad to help out, and I performed my kid-watching duty yesterday, so I was feeling confident putting the "Intimate Sailing" notion in my shopping cart. But it was not going to the sales register. Although my kids finally decided to stay with their grandparents and fish from the pier, freeing us, I was too late to hip my mermaid that sailing was a "go." She had already decided to rejoin Wayne and the Frogmen for another sea hunt for "low vulnerability" bass [bass who are smarter than fishermen]. This time, a net was being made from string to assist in the kill. Not much brain, but some taut and tanned, male muscle was assembled in this group. I had to admit I was a bit jealous that she was choosing to be the lone female in a boat with three other men over sex sailing with me. I decided to go adventuring, too—fishing with Johnny in the shallow canoe. Destination: the small islands in the middle of the lake.

Johnny was happy to have me along, even though he understood fishing was never my first choice of things to do for enjoyment. It is said that fishing is just drinking with a fishing pole in your hand. In our case, it was drinking and passing a joint with poles in our hands. We paddled and drifted along the front of the closer island, but had no bites. After an hour or so of "no luck", we came to the bend of the island's edge and the point where a narrow divided this island from the next one. We decided to try our luck over there. Our luck did change. We paddled away about ten strokes when the calm water suddenly became choppy, the waves rapidly hitting the side of the canoe with some force. The narrow had become a race, and our canoe was getting T-boned by some pretty righteous waves that were building enough to swamp or flip us. I had a vague remembrance that we ought to point the canoe into the waves. That, or paddle as hard as we could for the other shore—and be quick about the choice. We were two poor swimmers, fully dressed, booted, and about to get rocked over into a cold lake. I turned to look at Johnny for reassurance, but I didn't get the Richard Pryor imitation, scared face. He was looking over the top of my head, and I detected concern in the voice of my dare devil brother.

"You better put your life-jacket on, Jack. Yeah, fuckin' do it. Get it on now."

"You got yours on? Where's yours?"

"No. You go first. Now! for Christ's sake." It was probably the first time I could remember him telling me what to do, other than to go fuck myself. That's when I knew we were in trouble. Another sign was that I heard myself say aloud:

"I wish I wasn't stoned."

Tokers just didn't say that very often. It didn't matter if they were suddenly forced to act straight—like when a parent showed up unexpectedly, or after getting a last minute call to substitute teach in the trade school—or perform a physical task requiring guts and balance and judgment, like driving a piece o' shit car to the Cape, or survive a fire fight with Viet Cong. In my direct and word-of-mouth experience, 999,999 times out of one million, the attitude of a toker was "It's going to be a trip to do this stoned." Naturally, this was true if you were listening to music, or having sex, or eating, doing anything pleasurable, but it could also be something nasty. This was that "one time in a million" for me.

Not wanting to be stoned was not a response to fear or getting busted, but a sadness that a good "high" was about to be wasted on hacking a mundane, uncool event. Surviving getting your line wet on a small lake was not heroic, funny, clever or anything to talk about. It was stupid to be in this situation. The results I envisioned were, at best, a humiliating escape; at worst, suffering a regrettable death. I didn't want my senses elevated for either event. So I wished I was straight for whatever we had coming.

What we had coming was pre-determined, our fate cast, and our pot luck selected from the moment Johnny took the stern seat, becoming the "driver" of the canoe. Or, it could be said that Mr. Shelton's choice, three years ago, of an easy-to-control, short canoe with a wide beam had everything to do with how we managed to avoid capsizing. Maybe that and Johnny's years of playing the piano, strengthening his forearms and shoulders, saved the day. I only knew it had little to do with me or anything I did or had done. But this episode

181

of having to pivot the canoe "on command", at the precise moment the waves began to briefly slow, and then paddle with all the muscle we could muster in a desperate sprint toward shore, left me feeling less irritable about the food, a lack of sexual action, and not having a tan.

Reaching the first island again, we collapsed our arms over the canoe's gunwales and began to rest. Noise from across the water caught our attention. Lulu's off-pitch voice, thick blond pigtails, and short, cut-off jeans could not be ignored or mistaken even from half way across the lake. She was with a number of our group at the beach. Some of the clan was on the diving raft. Johnny and I thought it would be cool to paddle over there and get some sun if we could tone down the Lou-Lou experience an octave.

The farther we paddled in, the more we detected angry stares and bad vibes directed at our party from the straight people on the beach. Lusty disgust was the attitude shooting out from the nearest rowboat. Outgoing as he was, Johnny wanted to get a little closer to the boat and our floating voyeurs. We were only a few yards from the boat, which had one older guy and two teenagers, maybe his sons, aboard. They didn't seem to notice us as they were intently staring at the beach. Johnny got my attention with a poke of his paddle, motioning for me to hand him my binoculars.

"Hey, dudes! Checkin' out those chicks on the beach? Check the one in the cut-off shorts. Couple others look pretty do-able -- nice legs with tube tops, under blond hair. Oh, yeah...faces are there, too. Dark haired one's lookin' all set, man."

They turned together to look at us. The sight of Johnny's Crazy-the-Clown expression, psycho-killer hair and eyes, nicely set off my collegiate bomber look with John Lennon sunglasses and Walrus moustache. You could almost see our Jolly Roger run up their spines and out their bulging eyes.

"Have a real good look." Johnny said as he offered the closest boater the binocs, "We've seen them all before," he waved, "They're our sisters and girlfriends."

The older guy began a stammering explanation about "harmless observation...concern for safety on the diving dock," when a wriggling, bloody fish, impaled on a spear, shot out of the water between our canoe and the boat. Then another spear, and another, with snorkel heads bobbing up right after them. One of the young guys threw a life jacket at a snorkel head. The other raised the boat's anchor as the older guy started fumbling with the oars on an effort to row away. They were in freaked-out retreat. Ritchie raised his mask, looking around, laughing and snaring the life jacket with his spear. Wayne started talking about the amazing fight the little catfish put up in the water. The snorkelers had just lived a new adventure and weren't paying attention to the boaters. Suddenly, a booming voice was raised above all the noise.

"Drop it son! You heard me. Put the anchor down now or you'll all be placed under arrest," It was Fish & Game Warden, Johnny, clenching his shining badge, thrusting his arm toward the teenager's eyes, stopping any idea the young man might have had about throwing the anchor at someone. He dropped anchor... in the boat...silence.

"Now keep rowing or I'll make a complete safety inspection of your craft and cite the owner for any violations." Almost a minute went by before our laughter spread across the water, some of it directed at the boaters, some in honor of Johnny's latest rendition of a person in authority, and a good portion supported by Wayne's "kill" of a foot-long bottom feeder. Even Wayne had to laugh at his surprised discovery of the fish's power and courage, but nobody was up for taking it off the spear prongs, except the Lake Man, Mark. The rest of us begged off.

"Those fins can cut ya' pretty deep...bad infection if that top fin gets ya'... Back off, stick. I don't want its slime on my hands..." and other cop-outs were heard when it came down to a one-on-one with the little fighter. I immediately declared that I would not eat it.

My epiphany after the near drowning had not lasted very long. Sex being my next concern, I looked for the "Posada" boat and my wife. I soon spotted the boat, the chalet name in blue across the stern. But I didn't see a brunette with a sizeable, natural life jacket in the boat. I called out a couple times and, finally, Carly's bust with sunglasses askew, popped up. She had been sun bathing, "top on" I believed, while the hunters were patrolling for bass. Johnny and I gave Carly a ride to the pier, leaving the boat at anchor for the whale hunters. On the paddle home, while Johnny related the events of the last couple hours to Carly, I was silently thinking about how my kids were doing. Some of the concern was plain selfish: were they having a good enough time so they and my parents wouldn't mind if we just stopped in momentarily, grabbed a picnic basket, and moved on to the catamaran sail?

Then I began to feel the skin on my face becoming a little tight and a tinge hot. The sun stung my back...ah, the much desired pain of a tan being born. Sure, I was thankful for escaping the "ole' watery grave" but I was young enough to want more out of life than avoiding negatives. Sex under the potent sun, savory food, and a sinewy, bronzed body were desires worthy of the life force, and I had to experience them on this vacation while the sun shined and the girl was still mine.

The first piece to fall into place was safely occupying our kids, Rod and Rachael. Like most children, our physically challenged ones were utterly bored with the antics of the mother and father they loved, but wished to escape. Grandparents are well known for gladly filling the job of safety-minded, yet pliable, arms, legs, and minds in service to their grandchildren's fun time. All four were happy to see us, and still be happier to see us go. We only had to stop long enough for hugs, "thank you's" and me to pack up some cold chicken and pasta salad avec Scotch and pink Catawba.

As for Carly, I began to sense that she wasn't psyched for the sail ... certainly not for the same reasons I wanted to go sailing. Her mind was elsewhere, as if taking off on the lake wasn't that important to her, or maybe my being on the sailboat wasn't really required. She agreed to go, but when someone asks: "Since when do you like to sail? Do you know how? What's everybody else doing?" and they know damn well you have ulterior motives, it [pardon me] takes the wind out of your sails. Maybe that was the desired effect. Possibly, she wanted an innocent vacation away from me and I was supposed to read that message and drop the idea.

But I'm afraid I disappointed. My senses of pride, of courtesy, especially complacency, were no-shows. Floating intimacy with a good buzz goin' was not a gross-out. I knew from grad school rumors that female graduate assistants were joyously logging more sailing time on Narragansett Bay than the entire class at the Newport Naval War College; and not with rich fiancés-- with deans old enough to be their grandfathers. Yet, here I stood in my madras Bermudas, halter-style Frye boots, and wife beater tee-- a mini-Apollo in rut-- without a promise. I couldn't accept that this Indian maiden before me, who was always right in synch with my vibe, was not turned on by the getaway cruise idea. This part of the plan—her desire, not just agreement—was supposed to be a given. But I was sex-deprived enough to settle for "agreement."

She quietly stepped onboard, but vows or no vows; I could never accept marital sex. The appetizer and dessert mood changers were in the picnic cooler. The main course was the bag of herbal magic tucked in my boot [you can't hide a dime bag in Topsiders]. I was positive that after a drink or two and some salad, we would start a joint. The first effect might be a thought in her mind, or maybe a feeling in her heart. At some point, the weed would concentrate the flow of her chi in her sacred, lower tantien and change her from a merely agreeable partner into an urgent case of horniness demanding carnal satisfaction from me.

I had to bear in mind the low-side to the high-side. Getting stoned would not help me handle the boat thing. It was true: I didn't like sailing, rarely went sailing, and didn't know how to sail. But we found that floating was alright, providing a gently continuous rhythm that reminded me of the name of the infamous pick-up drink—"A Long, Slow, Screw"-- wicked romantic. Extra credit points: floating on a catamaran doesn't take much effort or care—and if you believe that—you can feel free to tune out the day's hassles, inhale nature, relish the taste of a summer lunch, and get loaded without minding the boat.

Cocktails and lunch had their desired effect. It was time to light a fatty. But I didn't carry matches since I had quit smokes. Carly always had matches in her bag. And that saved the day...and the good time, because there's nothing like balling on weed to the roll of waves. Sure, there was mounting evidence that a sloppy couple could bend a boner during sex-ahoy, but the growing demand for waterbeds was going mainstream because of its sexual effects. Forget the "bad back" smokescreen. The massive hot water bottle in a bed frame created more bad backs than they helped, according to the people I knew who had one. They also caused their owners to have more surprise company than the first color TV's. These sexually lazy, "tight friends," dressed in bathing suits or PJ's, would bop over, smoke some of the host's shit, drink the house wine, act sleepy and ask if they could nap on the water bed. After a few visits, the "guests" would be asking for condoms and a wake-up call, with phone and kid silence during their "nap". Things became a radical hassle when a dude would show with a different lady than the first one, and vice versa. Aiding and abetting adultery was a highly prized criminal conviction in the Pilgrim State.

Right then, I was buzzed, moving with the flow that was carrying my body toward hers, my hand holding out the joint for her to take another hit but gliding by her outstretched arm, letting my chest fall into the space between us, my lips faintly touching the side of her neck, feeling her arm around my back, pulling me in, stinging my sunburn [fuck it] as I put the joint out in the water and brought my hand to the side of her breast and my mouth up to her lips, kissing them, then down to her nipple, pulling it slightly up between my lips, feeling it harden there as she slid her hand into my shorts, caressing --BAM! Who put a boulder near the shore? She reactively clenched my balls, I bit her nipple, and the pasta salad-in-Tupperware was thrown into the water. Our speeding, pleasure transmission was thrown into reverse gear.

I didn't pass out, but I sensed a dimming of the

187

bright sun and a slight chill. It was just a passing pillow cloud. Then the breeze became a wind. Looking around the deck, all our clothes were on board. The cooler was still there. Carly's book and my cassette player both present. Where were the paddles? No paddles? Then I saw one paddle, lashed to one of the hulls. That was it, we had only one paddle. What good was that? For one thing, it was a good weapon to keep the honking, male swan, who abruptly sprang from the tall grass, from bill butting us for messing around to close to his nest. I kept Carly behind me as I used the paddle to push off the boulder and then delivered one good slap on the water to give him pause about trying to catch up to us.

But one paddle wouldn't drive this cat in a straight line. That was a problem because the wind direction and was taking us farther down the lake and away from the Posada. Without two paddles, I couldn't cave in, drop the sail and free both of us to row to the pier. I decided to raise the sail and try to tack against this wind. But I didn't know how to tack; only what it meant. Unimpressed by my efforts to zigzag with any speed, Carly suggested we "swim" the boat back home. Never heard of that method, but we knew how to do it. It was a grind and killed what was left of our energy, taking more than an hour to reach the pier. The effort killed what remained of our buzz, too. But the swim gave her sunburn on her back to balance the one on her front. I ended up looking like a Red Devil fishing lure: red on the back, white on the belly. I'm lucky a big bass didn't strike me. Luck, or I was considered too bony for a decent meal.

We cleared our stuff off the boat, secured it to the pier, and ached for awhile. Once we could walk, we started for the small beach to check on our kids. Looking ahead, we could see a bunch, maybe more like a mob, of people heading toward us, their noise reaching us before we made a visual I.D. of them. It was our beach goers, trudging along the wide path near the shoreline, dragging coolers, kids, and wet towels. They were escorted on the lake side by the fish hunters in boat and canoe. I wondered whether it was too much sun that drove them toward the shade of home base, or the herding skills of my sisters, who may have decided to start the evening meal early so that Ma and Pa wouldn't leave for the camper without first having a good dinner. Carly and I had a heart-skip moment when we saw Rod and Rach traveling in Uncle Johnny's canoe, hanging their chests over the gunwale, looking in the water. Normal heart beat returned when we saw they were wearing little life jackets. The exact type of approved life preserver they would never put on for us. Uncle Johnny was expert at conning little kids. I realized that made two surprises in one day and there's a proverb about things coming in three's.

Holy Labor Day! The cooks, including Carly, had secretly planned a clam and lobster bake for the getaway meal. Maybe that's where her attention was when mine was between my legs... or her legs. Eddie had snuck out for the lobsters, carrying precise instructions from lobster connoisseur, Wayne, on how to select the best "bugs". Wallets were opened, coolers were commandeered for lobster limo's, and the good times rolled, as did the joints, and we started early enough to still be standing as Ed and Betty pointed the New Yorker towards New York, destination: home, South Wheelbarrow, Massachusetts. Suzanne had the chalet to look after and I had the job of keeping the neighbors from harm, as well as preparing the grounds to look, smell, and sound like a quiet camp of eight to ten people—just to cover a surprise visit by a neighbor, the owner, or cops with real badges.

The next day, a surprise visit did go down. But not made by any of the above. It was early riser, Eddie, and sleepy, coffee addict, Betty. They were supposed to spend a day at home before returning to the chalet. But, here they were, right back with the camper--a full day early. Many of us were still in post-party repair. The worst cases I had moved to the "hangover tent" Joey and Mark pitched in the small meadow, away from the chalet. Liz, Caroline, and Laura were deputized as nursing orderlies by actual RN, Lulu. They worked in rotation, re-hydrating and goofing on those who overdid until they were recovered enough for their eyes to glimpse the sunlight and their stomach able to hold steady against the growing smell of garbage from the bake. The lobster shells reeked like aged "sick baby" diapers and, I strongly believed, were the real reason the native peoples buried them. Their use as fertilizer was an unexpected bonus. Another bonus: this aggressive, but totally legal, stench would cover the comparatively mild aroma of an illegally overrun septic system. A good thing, if the owner or city inspector made the scene.

"I thought you guys were gonna continue the party after we left." Coming from my father, this comment was a rare compliment that we did our duty and picked up the place before crashing. But we didn't plan on sobering up so soon. "Things look pretty well in order. Any smell yet, or visible overflow?" He noticed the lawn bags still scattered around the yard and picnic tables, "Better get those bags over to the dump."

"Trust me Dad; we need them right where they are. We do have some sewage smell. The stink of the shells in those bags masks that smell and, if the owner comes today, it'll keep him inside the chalet—where you want him to be."

After a quick nose hit, he winced like he'd been slapped across the face. Then he nodded in agreement. "Since we don't have to do much here, I figure a group of

190

us oughta' take a ride around the nearby area for a trailer camp."

"I think that's a good idea, Dad, but I ought to stay here if you and Ma go. Carly, the kids, and I should be here to greet the owner if he drops by."

"Well, he is coming," my father said as though I should have known this, "I called him this morning and he's heading up here as soon as he can leave work—sometime around 2:00. Be here by 4:00, he guesses."

"Then I'd better plan on being here and you guys can figure out how to spread everybody else around so there's only six or eight of us here at the chalet. We number twenty-eight kickin' around right now. I think you should get some bodies over to the beach and maybe put a foursome out fishing on the lake. There are four people chillin' in the tent...pretty quiet group, not ready for sailing. They can stay hidden there. If you and Ma take the camper and a following car with six people in it, that would get the number here down to eight. What do you think?"

"Don't see why not. But we have to get moving before people start using the toilet and sinks. Betty!"

"What is it, Ed, raccoons in the stinky garbage?" she rasped, drawing on some ultra-long, low tar cigarette.

"See if Mama Suzanne can get six people together to come with us to find a campground. We need to get going before the owner shows up, OK?"

And soon, the camp searchers were on the road, sunbathers were at the public beach, away from the neighbors, and the fishermen were drinking in boats at a good distance from our shore. We had the oldest and most responsible-looking types inside the chalet playing Scrabble with my kids. Carly, Young Eddie and I were sitting on the front porch, confidently waiting for the landlord.

We had some time on our hands and, I thought, what better way to spend it than to try rekindling the lusty mood we had on the catamaran before hitting the stone berg. After asking Eddie if he wouldn't mind keeping watch alone, we were off to the Bridal Suite. This was a radically different scene than the al fresco setting we had the day before, but it had its own charm and we were quickly back to the part where we hurt our parts.

She had another perfect looking breast for me to use, but I could only offer the "scratched and dented" model of my bag of fun. We were working carefully around those areas when I began to hear two voices in conversation. Carly heard them, too. One voice was Eddie's. The other was a new voice, a polite voice--the owner. Whether expected or not, this was yet another interruption, to be followed by another challenge to act straight. My self-pity was heavy. What a rip-off! We weren't under-aged kids who needed saving from sin and pregnancy, or a wayward couple committing adultery and deserved disappointment. We were legally married, happy young hippy freaks who needed sex to keep the counter- culture going. But a higher duty called.

Carly and I dressed and went to the porch to meet The Man. He looked like an old math teacher in his worn, tweed sport coat, pale complexion and neat crew cut. He was no pot head, for sure, but his tone of voice and manner said he was a pleasantly quiet guy who seemed to lack the assertiveness I associated with people who regularly enforce rules and collect money ... like teachers, and landlords who rent out chalets to strangers. Looking across at my brother, I was surprised to see they were having an enjoyable conversation. Eddie, with his hair all freaked out, bloodshot eyes; dressed in the pothead denim uniform, and this soldier in the straight life, had plenty to argue about, lots of areas of contention. What had they found agreement on? I doubted it was the number of occupants here, which was the reason for the visit. They were so wrapped up; I had to interrupt their conversation to call our little meeting to order.

"Wanna beer, bro?" Eddie asked from the frig door.

"I've got a scotch. Why don't you ask Mr. Shelton what he would like to drink?"

"That's who I'm asking, Big Jack. I could see you had your scotch and Carly's got her pink vino. Guests first, right Carly?" Eddie asked. Carly nodded, in response.

"A beer would be fine, Ed...no glass, thank you." replied our landlord.

Something was definitely up. Young Ed was taking me to task on manners, calling our potential hook man "bro", and acting like the cat that swallowed the canary. Things were going fine, actually. The guy wasn't yelling and demanding to look under every bed—which I half-expected. But I had to take charge. I always felt like I had to take charge.

"My father's not here right now, Mr. Shelton, but he spoke with you on the phone earlier, right? Something about your neighbors complaining to you, concerned about how many of us are here. Am I correct?" I asked.

"I have a copy of the Newbridge paper here, and it reports the neighbors' have many concerns. They notified me and I was about to call your father when he called me first thing this morning. He said I could talk to you; that he'd be looking for a campground, so he could move some of your party out of here. Your brother says there are sixteen family members sleeping here, which are six or eight above the maximum I advertized. It's not that I mind creative bunking, so to speak. The problem is in the bathroom... it's the town's waste water code."

"And the neighbors have reported him to the town before, once when only six people were here. They're out to drive you out-- right Harry? Eddie shot into the discussion. And now I was beginning to see what the private conversation was about.

"Let's just say that the obvious spying, body counting, and noise complaints have been going on since I bought this place and fixed it up." Mr. Shelton continued, "Some of the so-called neighbors live at the other end of the lake! But they are part of a group of lake front owners who simply don't want me to feel comfortable renting the chalet. I still rent it, because that's how I'm able to afford it. So, I have to make sure the party does not exceed the limits, or somebody will report it. And if the town engineer determines that renters are stressing the waste system, I can be fined and prohibited from renting...which could cost me the chalet. In the short run, your entire party would have to leave."

"I'm sorry we gave them another opportunity to hassle you, Mr. Shelton. We are a large family, and we know what it's like to have neighbors in your face, but some times we naturally react with a few wicked stares of our own. I'm sure that added to their complaints. But if I hear you, we're still cool to stay, as long as eight of us move out to a campground or somewhere else?" I asked.

"That's right. And, don't worry about the neighbor's attitude as long as you keep the number of

194

people here to eight sleepers, ten total people at any given time. Pretty soon I won't have to be concerned about this closed-minded community. The other reason I came up here was to sign papers with a realtor. I'm putting La Posada up for sale; not only over this sewage issue, but the rental picture. This area hasn't had enough natural snow for the last three years to sustain quality skiing. Solid rental bookings have dropped to sporadic, at best. You can't make up for it in the summer. Well, that's my problem. I'd better get going. Thanks for the beer, Ed.

Mr. Shelton shook our hands and walked to the door. "Say 'Hello' to your Mom and Dad. I wish I had a chance to meet them today, but I'll be staying in town for another day or so if he wants to give me a call. I'll be at this number."

After he was gone, I asked Eddie what was happening with him and Shelton in the private conversation.

"He asked me if I knew what the name of the chalet meant. You know, the signs all around the place: La Posada on the mailbox, over the doors, the deck post—all over. I said 'No, I didn't, but maybe my brother does because it sounds Spanish and he knows a little Spanish. Harry said it's not Spanish. It's Portuguese for 'Place of Peace'. They have a Christmas thing in Portugal where each house in the neighborhood takes a turn during the season be the 'Shelter and Place of Peace', La Posada, for the other neighbors. The Posada house throws a big meal and gives small gifts to everyone. It's like taking turns being the stable and manger for Baby Jesus.

Well, Harry and his friend visited one of these celebrations over there and he got the idea of having his own shelter, a place to get away from the job hassles and

195

people in his family who don't dig his partner thing. So he bought this chalet and named it La Posada. But once the neighbors figured out his sexual persuasion, they became hostile fuckers. He told you the rest, brotha."

"That's a shame," said Carly, "Why should it bother them that he's a homosexual? That makes him some sort of criminal? Is it like living next door to a thief or a murderer or someone like that? To each his own, I always say."

"Speaking of which, we each need a place to eat and sleep by tomorrow. I hope the crew can find a good campground that doesn't have an occupancy limit. It's looking like the family's getting too big for a vacation together. We've got five families inside the Family; and it's going to get bigger when one or two more sisters get married in the next couple of years. How and where are we going to go then? Rent two chalets next to each other and three campers, surrounded by a dozen tents?" I asked Carly.

We were growing, but not wanting to grow outward—move out to some other state, or even another town. We grew up together and wanted to stay close together, where we could fight and complain, or support and help each other, depending on what the situation required, without a long drive or even a walk. And my parents were, or seemed, quite comfortable continuing as an integral part of everything we did, especially raising our children. Most other families got the hell away from each other as soon as possible, only to return for special events. We knew that, but we were always different from other families. Why stop now? Maybe we would have to, having reached a critical mass for family size in the suburbs of Twentieth Century America and, though we might stay living close by in different houses, vacations were different. Nobody wanted to start taking separate vacations, but it was sinking into my brain that we had gone well beyond the normal limits of group vacation arrangements.

The camp finders returned. They reported that the one place within a half-hour ride could take the camper with four people. An additional four would have to sleep in the large tent on a separate site. This would suck; dividing up food and probably family units, cars coming and going to get together for a shared activity. Our shared vacation would become a hassle fest of frustration. Even my father, the optimist inventor seemed a bit uncertain about pulling a great vacation out of these circumstances. Ma was a master at making a little go a long way, and although she had stretched the available space, she couldn't stretch the septic limits any longer, nor constipate twenty-eight people.

Our top problem solvers sat at the large dining table, staring off, outwardly calm while desperate ideas loudly collided within the "planning room" of their minds. A mouth moved to speak every so often, stopping with a strained exhale and a dejected head shake. Finally, a complete sentence from Carly:

"Jack and I have the opposite problem when we borrow my father's motor home. We can't make it sleep more people than it's laid out for, but there's never a worry about how many times we shower, or flush the toilet. The bathroom is barely big enough for a person to sit down. But my father says the tank holds enough water for six people to use it for a month."

Carly and I had taken that motor home about a dozen times and, she was right, we never worried about the blackwater tank filling up. Her father never mentioned it, and he had a list of things for us to worry about. We were totally drilled on running out of drinking water, or using up the batteries and then having to start the loud generator. But there was no limit on trips to the poop chute.

"Carly, would you mind giving your father a call? I need to ask him something about the motor home." And we excused ourselves from the table. "Can we use the phone in your room, Ma? Thanks. We'll be back shortly."

We used the phone in the deluxe bedroom, leaving the heavy thinkers to become happy drinkers in the dining room, and the stoners on the porch. Carly caught her dad at home and off the phone...a lucky break for us. He was continually talking to someone about old cars, or out somewhere checking out an antique car—his real job but not his official, "going to work", job. Carlton Smith liked to collect almost anything on wheels, including a tall-wheel unicycle he kept in his garage. Not the shiny circus thing-- the original, 1800's, five-footer, with a tiny wheel at the back. They called them "penny-farthings" after the British coins, one being large, the other very small, like the size of the two wheels. It required the rider to mount the seat from a set of backdoor stairs, a fence, or sturdy box. Only macho guys with handlebar moustaches and bowler hats were allowed to ride them. I guess the thinking was "If you're bodacious enough to grow that foot-long 'stache on your face and put that ridiculous hat on your head, then no one will be surprised, or miss you, if you kill yourself trying to ride over bumpy roads on a huge wheel." These dudes especially liked to ride them to the park on a Sunday, when everyone else was out and about. World War I put an end to most of this nonsense.

"Hi, Dad, it's me. How are things there? We're having a great time, but I guess there's too many of us to stay here any longer. Some of us might have to move out to a nearby campground... Yeah, we have Mr.

198

Prudhomme's trailer camper...I think that's what Jack wants to ask you about. Here he is. I'll talk to ya' later."

"Hi Dad, let me ask you something..."

Smitty answered all my questions and had a few of his own. He and Carly's brother, Andy, were about to leave for Stowe, Vermont, and the major Antique and Classic Car meet that's held there every summer. He talked about maybe going a little off course to visit us for an afternoon. I told him that would be cool, without checking with Central Control. But there was no need to ask. Besides being family, Carlton Smith was a showman, and Ed and Betty always loved to have a visit from the Swing dancer, comedian, and storyteller. Furthermore, as a former Navy comedian, he always had a grass skirt and hugely padded bra stowed away somewhere "on board" and was known to suddenly change in to it, or arrive dressed in it, complete with wig, hairy chest, and ukulele. No one would question the opportunity to see that kind of live entertainment.

Yet, I did have questions for Central Control and for Mr. Shelton. Since we were going to have to split up in to two groups, I would be loosely in charge of one group and needed to know what the plan would be for daily communication, shopping, cars, the whole shebang. Carly was good at keeping all the details straight and Mama Suzanne would enforce wherever enforcement was needed, God help them. With kids involved, we needed some order to our chaos.

Before dinner I had all I needed to know about our vacation's future bed and bath possibilities. By morning, I was tanning my front parts lying atop Smitty's motorhome, which slept seven and toileted twice that many for over a week before the tank needed "dumping". La Posada was now more like the genuine,

Portuguese neighborhood version. The chalet was still the primary place to sleep, eat, and hang out. But, several yards away, sitting on the owner's vacant lot, we now had a state of the art "home on wheels" with 360 degree views of nature. A short distance from it, the camper-trailer looked kinda passé—nothing attractive or new about it. But that made it positively interesting during the day since there was nothing to do there but go to bed.

We would continue to be under surveillance by the lake club crowd, but we were still there together, in different shelters close enough to gather for a meal, duck into for a secret nap, or hale over some rowdy company. And we didn't have to pay Smitty a dime, not even for the beaucoup gas he used getting here and then taking his towed Caddy over to Stowe in the middle of the night. Still, I needed a tan by nightfall to look decent for keeping my bargain with him. Hula "girls" never wear glasses, but they always have perfect tans.

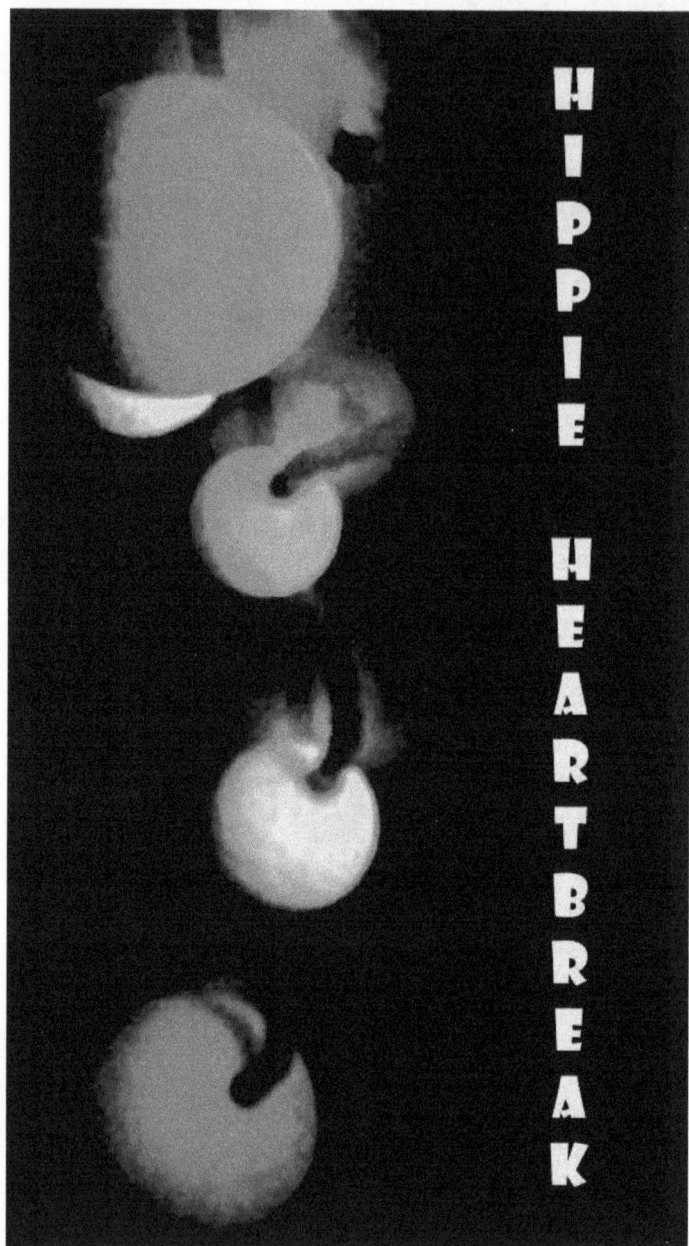

HIPPIE HEARTBREAK

I spent yesterday at the beach not far from my Gulf-facing condo in St. Pete. After five years here, escaping from five frosty decades spent in New England, I've noticed changes taking place in paradise. The dependably warm and sunny weather, accessible, white beaches, palm trees, and calm, blue water all remain as stunning as when we first visited. The change has been a wave of 60's "stuff" continually lapping the shores of the everyday scene. I'm seeing "Hippies" everywhere. Not the Hippies, not my hippies, but a number young and recently young people wearing Frank Zappa's face on their tees and making other personal freedom statements with their appearance. These teen to late 20's people are diggin' the fashions, lifestyles, and social concerns of the 60's Counter-Culture. This may have resulted from their recent discovery of a few mutually appealing turn-ons we indulged in four decades ago.

Naturally, there are slight changes from the 60's. For instance: our music never left, but now it is re-mixed, digitized, and often covered by a younger artist. Hair statements aren't universally about long hair, but often absent of hair; or short and precisely messed up; sideburns are 'in' again, but they're skinny. Sorry, back hair is still 'not cool'. Bras are not burned, but panties are optional; and the re-designed, bell-bottomed hip huggers are, more accurately, pubic bone markers. Show me your tattoo? Forget about it! There's more than several in direct view and they're worn by all teams. Groovy, again, is sex with someone you just met. Only now it should occur in a dangerously public place, not just in the meadow, or a friend's pad. Time demands adjustments. Still, the dynamic of the 60's movement, rebellion, can be found in these edgy, shocking appearances and sexual mores. Yesterday, I heard the word "rebellion" seriously used in a TV commercial. A young man gave me the peace sign when I let him cross the street. People are acting cool again.

Where there's rebellion and conflict, there's fire and smoke.. And that is why the more I see protesters and feel rebellion in the air, the more bongs appear and more weed I smell. It's in the movies, and on TV, in the news, and celebrated in song. It is everywhere, all the time. At first, not expecting a hemp revival with all the meth labs popping up, I thought I smelt some kind of Florida sea weed. But it was Tex-Mex weed. And just as "turning on" in the 60's started a chain reaction of rejection of the status quo and discovery of ancient new ideas, so now I saw a handful of war protestors sharing the Bay Way meridian with the ever-present homeless beggars. On weekends, these separate groups often find themselves sharing the same high-traffic corners with the high school car washers and the newspaper vendors. Though in competition for space and attention, I have observed them eventually finding mutual acceptance and support as they shout across to each other. Even the French Revolution didn't unite such a diverse collection of partisans. Shared experiences like foul air and foul-mouthed drivers, etc., give them shared adversaries. And from that a chance to communicate with each other about shared problems. I'm feeling the vibes of the old Hippie "social consciousness" re-emerging along with the beads and pot smoking.

So I suppose we 1st edition Hippies should be happy and even proud that the trappings and ideals of our blitzed youth seem to be enjoying popularity with a new generation. Sad to me, personally, is that among my generation's counter-culture trappings, you will not find my attempt to be one of Zappa's Mothers of Invention. I created a jewel of mind-blowing, visual apparatus that completed the stoned experience. But its mass production got side-tracked, and evidence of its existence cannot be found. Actually, I can find it, because it's still in a large, black canvass bag in my tool closet. This innovation is an artistic device only a few have actually seen, but millions have glimpsed in its playful, visual essence. Those, still living, who have seen its effects, cannot forget it and the fun it created. It is the GlowRope. And its success fell victim to circumstances I shall explain.

For now, I wonder how today's "Hippie," the new toker, would react to the Glow Rope. But it was always a great show when you were high. It was designed for that state of mind. I don't "turn on" anymore, so I probably wouldn't be a good judge of the glowers' "wow" power with today's stoners. My wife, Carly, and I stopped getting buzzed decades ago. We developed a real-life, "Magic Dragon" problem: it just didn't fit into a busy day of work responsibility, teaching college, and raising our two barrels of monkeys, who depended on us for all kinds of things. Besides, as they got older, they could tell when we were high and would take advantage of us.

But there was a time when getting high every day and night was absolutely needed because it gave you a body-rush that blew away the day's hassles; freed the mind, and left you relaxed. This is not to mention how well it enhanced listening to music and "getting it on." Turning on was a brave, new experience, unlike anything else we had done; so captivating that everything else we did revolved around it. But after a year or so, continually getting wasted could get boring. To our horror, it became the normal state, not the escape place. So lava lights and black light posters, and other smoking "toys" found a market with us. Early stoners designed these things that quickly landed on the shelves of Hippie boutiques, then regular stores. They enjoyed good sales for years. Were today's bongers looking for a novel enhancement to their usual buzz? If Frank Zappa music, doing weed, casual sex, and social awareness were making a comeback, maybe the Glow Rope would finally emerge as the perfect visual effect for the mind and the senses.

As they direct on TV shows, "Go back 40 years." The idea of a glowing rope just popped into my head late one night when I realized I wasn't going to find happiness as a substitute teacher. Most people dream of doing something that combines their interests with their job. For me, this would be it: constructing and selling a black light-illuminated wave or spinning device that a person would be free to move and change in shape, creating visual images to intensify the stoner's "buzz." This idea formed out to become a prototype glower, consisting of a 4 ft. length of rope, running through carefully spaced, Day-Glo painted, Styrofoam balls of different sizes, weights, and colors. The player was able to gyrate this ball-studded rope like a lasso, swinging the balls in loops , circles, helixes, and spirals creating an amazing variety of glowing, spinning trails of colors that changed constantly in a 3-D, "mini-solar system."

With Carly's help and the financial backing of our tax refund of $230, I made a few of these glowers. I also took the design to my father's patent attorneys, Palter & Michaelson. I was optimistic to the point of worrying someone would rip-off my idea once it took-off. We sat down for a minute, then he asked about my father, Ed Prowse.

"How's he doing? I'm sure it must have been tough to get over. Your father had a sure winner with that safe diaper clasp invention. It could have made him a millionaire. Then the disposable diaper hit the market just ahead of him. Now the trash sites are full of shitty plastic diapers that won't go away for 5000 years."

I told him that despite the obvious disappointment, he's still a quiet, steady, optimistic Eddie.

"My dad quit welding and inventing. He signed

up to play piano with a jazz band on one of those cruise ships: a floating, all-you-can-eat restaurant and pick-up lounge. He'd be gone for a couple months at a time. Now he's thinking about moving way out...maybe California or Florida."

"As long as he's happy." Michaelson said as he opened my folder and started reviewing the notes and designs I sent to him. After he finished reading, he became very stone-faced, staring at the actual ropes. He declined to see the glowers in action. This surprised me. They impressed everyone in my circle who saw them and used them-- stoned or straight. I told him I had no doubt it would sell big.

"I've seen stranger things succeed," were his only words of encouragement.

"How could an old straight guy dig this?" I laughed to myself, "He's a good lawyer but he's not into our bag. Good thing I didn't come for praise or financial backing, just protection." I put up the bread for a title search, thanked him, and left.

News of the glowers' mind-blowing visuals got Carly and I invited to lots of parties and little get-togethers. Our home also had the honor of occasionally being invaded by friends and friends of friends, and sometimes just strangers my brother, Johnny, would find on the street or in coffee shops. The glowers were always a big hit after a few hits. We got to know how to work them pretty well for maximum effect. Reviews from partiers, like: "That's heavy, man," and "Far out," were kickin,' but rarely got us a sale. Money is a hard thing for most potheads to deal with while under the influence. If they have any money, they can't find it. If they can find it, they can't count it. By the time they count it, they forget why they counted it. But the positive reaction got us thinking we could amp up the sales numbers if we changed the target group. We decided to direct it at people with money to invest in mass production and marketing. Create a promotion more business-like, for people in business. Brilliant!

Before arriving at this decision we briefly played out a few other promotional strategies suggested by my friend, Kenny the Car Salesman. Please let me share a few with you:

Door-to-Door: "Good morning, Ma'am. May I speak with the pothead of the house?"

Business Drop-By: "Great topless place you got here, Mr. Big Al. You know, these girls can get pretty tired swinging around the same old pole all day. For a change of pace, maybe you could have them swing this painted rope with balls on it?"

Public Agency Support: "Listen, please, Chief Morrissey. Local TV stations shoot a fair amount of drug bust coverage right here in the station, correct? How hard would it be to just throw a couple of these glow ropes on the "confiscation table" for the cameras to pan with the bags of pot, heroin bricks, guns and money? I need some product recognition in the community and we could put a $1,000 street value on them...punch up the numbers for the raid, dig?"

They were all possible strategies, but selling the idea of the GlowRope to an established manufacturer in a related field carried the day. We decided to prepare a "straight-folk" demo we could bring to a toymaker, a smoke shop chain, or blacklight poster company. Luckily, we lived right near Tasbro Toys, and having family who even worked there, made the home of "USA Joe" the logical place for our first pitch. It would also be easier to find than some mill outside New York City.

Beforehand, some of the 'side effects' and other little concerns needed attention. First, the Glow Rope obviously required a black light...something for our customer to purchase separately. And while it was that special light that made the balls magic, it also reflected many things in the room in an ugly, garish way.

For instance: the distinct scars of acne wars on the faces in the audience were horrifyingly vivid to the stoned eye. Glowing dandruff and lint showed everywhere. Make-up appeared hideous on otherwise pretty faces. Colored clothes looked like camouflage and white clothes turned an eerie blue. Bleached-white eyes popped out on faces everywhere in the room. After a few minutes of twirling the ropes, dots of fluorescent color could be seen everywhere: on carpets, dogs, cats, pizza left in the open, and floating in drinks. Hands, shoes, hair, faces and your new Army Surplus jacket were all speckled with paint from the balls. After noticing this, people would slowly stop grooving and start freaking out ... until the regular lights went back on; revealing that the horror show was only temporary. All the gross-out was easily fixed with a flick of a switch, a vacuum and fresh wine. Truthfully, seeing yourself in black light was kind of a rush in itself.

We were nearly ready to set up meetings with possible buyers of my diamond idea. But the GlowRopes were not. The pioneering prototypes were looking kind of abused. Life on the road, through three towns, had taken their toll. They'd been bounced on the floor, hit against walls, whipped around people, and used to tie up dogs. They suffered from bruised balls, frayed ropes, and slipped knots. The deluxe and very expensive, fluorescent blacklight I traded two lids of Panama Red for was losing its wiring connections; and there were scratches on the tube. Fixing the glowers seemed harder than making them from scratch. But the new ones failed to look as good and spin as well as the originals. The new ones literally suffered from "Made by a Hippie on Friday." syndrome. So we primed the veteran glowers for demo duty and hoped for the best.

Believing all was finally in place, and after receiving Attorney Michaelson's report, clearing my application for a patent pending, I picked up my phone and called Tasbro Corporation for an appointment with Product Development. Thanks to Atty. Michaelson, I had the direct number to Mr. Stephen Tassenfeld, VP for PD, the Man, through whom all new ideas must pass. The receptionist startled me by picking up in less than one ring, causing my mind to launch into a millisecond of imagined caller-bashing from the Guardian of the Gate:

"Mr. Tasbro's office! Identify yourself, please! Are you represented by counsel? What is the reason for your call? Speak up, please! Mr. Tassenfeld is a very busy person. When! Not possible. Nothing free until December 12th, 2:00 p.m... Wear black pants, white shirt, and narrow tie. No long hair. No facial hair. No visible tattoos. Park in the lower employee's lot, at the back, near the attack-dog kennel. Good bye."

Yanked back into real time, I heard a soft, kind voice say "Good morning, Mr. Tassenfeld's office. My name is Elaine. May I help you?" After introducing myself and my reason for calling, she put me right through to Mr. T. He was very calm and listened attentively. Nothing like the Robber Baron I was expecting. He sounded young, but he was no Hippie. I suspected he suspected I was, after a brief description of the GlowRope and what it does for whom. Nevertheless, he was "very interested" to see it work and added that Tasbro was always on the lookout for new ideas. Plans were made for a demo in two weeks at 11:00 a.m., in Mr. T's conference room. Park in the reserved area. There would be refreshments. Would I need any A-V equipment? Another phone? I felt treated with respect and grace. "Cool," I thought, "radically good first choice. And it may be the only one I'll need."

Demo Day came, and I was ready. I was to be a young, happening Hippie genius disguised in entrepreneurial killer clothing. Carly trimmed my wavy hair and mustache, filed my nails, made sure I didn't slip and take a toke or carry in a joint, or smell like one. I wore the business man's colors: Navy sport jacket over white shirt and striped tie, with grey slacks, socks, and cordovan slip-ons. Because of limited funds, I also had to make this outfit work at an upcoming wedding of real freaky friends, so Carly cheated a bit with the Babson College look and bought the trim, Italian cut, single-button, textured blazer. The slacks were the beaucoup "in," Elephant width. French cuffs finished the shirt; the shoes' soles were slightly platform; and the tie was a healthy 3" wide.

We met in the plush, air-conditioned, reception office...just the two of us. We introduced each other. Steve was a short guy, like me, with thick, curly black hair. I figured him to be maybe ten years older than me. A captain of industry, he studied me from within his banker's suit and tie. But he had an openly curious face and he seemed impressed that a Hippie could achieve an Economics degree. When I told him I taught ancient history part-time at RIC, he directly asked what I wanted from a toy manufacturer. Before I could find an answer other than money, he suggested we go into the conference room and get the show on the road.

I remembered to explain how each glower was constructed and showed how they were spun in different ways, before turning off the room light. Then, he watched

210

quietly as I worked each one in the eerie glow of the black light. The entire demo seemed to take only two minutes, but I knew it was longer. He turned on the lights, and then I saw it...a smile across his face. A few moments passed as he seemed to be thinking through all he had seen.

"Jack, could you leave one rope and the black light with me for a couple of days?" he asked, "I would like to show this to my research staff and take some pictures to run by the legal department. But I want you to know I liked it very much, quite entertaining."

I wanted to tell him to keep it a week or forever if he wanted to pay me for the rights to make them. The trouble was I had another demo with WallArt, Inc. in two days and no money for another long black light, even if I could find one. So I told him the truth, which he either believed, or he thought was a pretty ballsy bluff to get an answer right then and there.

"Alright, let's talk business right now, if you would like. You designed it and you have the rights to it. You have identified a segment of our consumer public who would buy it. Naturally, you don't want to miss an opportunity to find a buyer. So I'll say this 'off the record' before you see anyone else: I want to make the light. And I'll make you a formal offer after we pass it around the department. But I'm thinking my offer would be this: with Tasbro taking all the risk of production, I would want to own all the rights in exchange for giving you a % of sales and a selling bonus. If sales are better than expected, we would agree to re-open for stock in Tasbro. I think that would be a generous offer that could easily work out to more than, say, ten years of teaching college."

Good thing I wasn't stoned. I was having enough trouble quickly absorbing this offer with a clear head.

211

"Thank you. I'll think it over while you look it over," I replied as I put the light and a couple of ropes on the table.

"Elaine will call you with the time for our next meeting, Jack," Mr. T said as he walked me to the door, "Nice meeting you." And he shook my hand.

I started some heavy daydreaming while driving home about how my life would change with this imminent success. At first, it was all good dreams-- affording pot, taking Carly to expensive restaurants, lavishly entertaining friends and family, new houses for our parents, paid college for us and our brothers and sisters, massive Christmas parties, traveling, restoring and driving old Jaguars over the toll bridge to Newport beaches on Tuesday afternoons. Maybe I'll bleach my hair blond. Lots of stuff that only lots of money can make real.

Then it hit. The negatives: what if all this quick money led to changes we didn't want, like Carly leaving the kids with a nanny to go shopping all day somewhere; friends too stoned all the time to be funny anymore; greed and jealousy over every gift; constant watching over your back for the stranger at the party who's out to rip you off; bad vibes from folks you had to turn away; more people to take care of, and more problems to solve. No time to lie wasted on the sofa on a lazy afternoon just watching the kids play. What if wealth ruined my life?

My head was spinning, I was getting wicked paranoid of success without being on drugs. I could see everything dear to me becoming spoiled and I hadn't even made a single penny. Not one cent richer, and here I was falling apart behind the wheel. I could hear my mother's warning about money and it being the root of all evil, the seducer of your soul that would never provide peace of mind despite all it could buy. Better to be poor and honest, friendly and befriended, loved and welcomed rather than rich and despised, your happiness begrudged, and your goodwill mistrusted.

"Whoa! Get it together, man! Rein yourself in: the GlowRope was a happy toy, not a weapon. It brought laughter, not tears. And if I made money from it, why would that have to change everything, or anything, for the worst. If your heart's in the right place, you can control wealth for doing good, no downside necessary," I reassured myself.

So I returned home, happy to tell Carly the good news. And I told her not to let any negative thoughts in...I already took that trip, and came to see this deal would be a good thing for us. We'll use this money for positive things, and we'll always enjoy it.

We couldn't sleep that night until morning. We spent the rest of the day discussing different counter-proposals like: more up-front cash-- less % of sales; minimal cash--big % of sales; up-front cash, immediate stock shares and a lifetime cushy non-job with a generous expense account, company house and car. Round and round we'd go. The final truth was: whatever we got, it would be much more than what we had.

On the third morning, the phone rang. It was Elaine. I expected she was calling to give me a time and place for the big meeting. Instead, it was a quick "Hello, Jack," then a request to hold for Mr. Tassenfeld. He began to speak and the tone of his voice made my throat dry and my eyes feel heavy.

"Mr. Prowse, [what happened to 'Jack'?] I had hoped to be calling with a positive response to buying

213

your rope...make an appointment to discuss terms, and so forth. Unfortunately, there is a problem, sort of a health problem, with the use of the black light. This is from our legal department. They have a record of an accident with a previous toy of ours that was painted and used with a black light. I wasn't here then, so I was not aware of this incident until late yesterday," he explained at a slightly rapid, but carefully measured pace.

"What kind of accident?" I broke in, " I mean, did someone get a shock, or a fire break out? Those things are simply accidents. You're not scared off by..."

"It's the use of the light itself, Jack," he cut back in, sounding a bit frustrated at me, or maybe the whole situation, "The light changed the color of our salesman's skin. It happened in Canada. She was showing a wooden, toy train with the black light shining on it. We're not sure what, but something in the rays turned the woman's skin a silvery black. Or, was she black and her skin turned pearly white? Anyway, we were sued and eventually settled out of court for a large sum of money. And we lost the money we invested in the development of a complete line of black light toys."

"That accident could have been Mercury poisoning," I protested, "Really! My mother had a chemistry teacher at Hope High whose skin was silvery gray from getting mercury into a cut. It's a one-time thing that..."

"I love your idea, Jack," he interrupted, "But with this problem, I wouldn't touch it with a ten-foot pole. Not if it needs a black light. Sorry, Mr. Prowse. I know you had high hopes. So did I. But, it's too risky. I'll mail your equipment to you. "

That was the end of the discussion and the end of

the deal.

We went back to our Wheaties and wept. It was a good thing we didn't tell many people about our upcoming fortune, because that would have increased the humiliation and the time to tell people what had happened. Like when your wife is pregnant. You keep it quiet until everything looks like a sure "go."

I tried other toy places, but they weren't the least interested, black light or not. Poster companies were not geared for assembly or construction. Kenny the Car Salesman's ideas were still there, but too time-consuming and sporadic. So, I just put it away, except for our own amusement. It never changed our skin color, or our fortune. Maybe the poor woman was one in a million, but it was a million we wouldn't see. Maybe pot and being lucky didn't go together.

It's forty years later. Now, there's day-glow everything, from jump ropes to soccer balls, and black lights sold everywhere. So far, I have not seen one silvery or pearly skinned person...except at Mardi Gras. So it might be worth another try now that everything is 60's again. Seeing glow-effect ads on TV of teens dancing with a very popular, very small audio player connected to their ears, caused me to make up a dozen new glowers. Then I bought a display-grade, fluorescent, black light for them. I checked with another lawyer to renew my patent pending--all good. This time I checked for potential demand and any competition on the internet, not at parties. On the downside, with so many different glow gadgets for sale, I saw the market for day-glo was saturated. There was no GlowRope, but the manufacturers out there didn't see a need for one, either. I called around from Massachusetts to China. Again, we were on our own to make it and sell it.

We were still thinking it over when Carly spotted an ad for a Sixties Night Gala at a hotel on Gulf Boulevard. They welcomed 60's dress, cars, memorabilia, etc.. Music by some DJ. What the hell? We decided to go. At least we could dance to some tunes, have a few drinks, and people watch. We brought the black bag along, just in case.

It was a big, noisy crowd of all ages, not just old longhairs. The smell of weed hung in the air as Jimi Hendrix blared across the ballroom. The deejay was up on a low platform, scanning the audience, asking people up to display their outfit or tell a Woodstock tale. Soon, he zeroed his attention on us for some reason, maybe our dancing...we could still Monkey, Watutsi, whatever. He got us over to the mike, and asked what we did in the 60's. "Any stories?" [I know... If we remember anything, we weren't in the 60's.] Well, without missing a second, Carly's into it:

"We invented a glowing rope with different colored balls on it that blew your mind under a black light. And when you were high, you spun it around making wicked nice trails. Better than Orange Sunshine..."

"You still have one?" he asked before Carly made a complete confession of felonious possession.

"Sure!" Carly answered, "We have a couple with us if anybody wants to see them in motion," She turned to the crowded dance floor, "Anybody blitzed here?!"

This question brought loud yells, hoots, and general support for a GlowRope performance. We jogged out to the car, considered leaving, but grabbed the ropes and lights instead and returned to the stage for an impromptu GlowFest. Must say it went very well,

216

considering the small area where we could concentrate the black light. We did three songs with the ropes. After finishing, people surged forward to look at the ropes and talk to us. That's when this older guy rushed over and quickly stole us from the crowd with an offer of drinks and a table with chairs. He said he just wanted a quick conversation about the ropes.

"Thanks for joining me. I'm Jim Fromme," he said. "I really dig these ropes you've got here. I'm into 60's things. Got a big collection of all kinds of Hippie stuff. Never saw anything exactly like these, though. Do you sell many of them?"

"Actually, no, we didn't. But we will now!" I laughed. Then there was a pause. "We tried to start a business making these "in quantity" back then...in the late 60's... but it didn't work out. We still own the rights to the design, though. Excuse me, Jim. The "we" is us... my wife, Carly," I turned to introduce her, "and I'm Jack Prowse."

"Glad to meet you. Prowse, you said? I wonder, would your father's name be Ed, Eddie Prowse?" he asked in a hopeful way.

"Yeah," I replied, a bit surprised, "Yeah, My father's Eddie Prowse. He's a musician. You know him?"

"Know him? I sure do. You know he plays piano and bass on cruise ships most of the year. Well, I've been on more than a few cruises over the years. And on several, your father has been with one of the bands. Everybody calls call him 'Show Biz'. He laughs at that, because there's nothing showy or glitzy about him. Am I right? He sticks to his job. Has a very nice touch on bass, but never looks for special attention. He wants the other guys, especially the "young" guys {in their 40's}, to take their twenty bars, have a solo spot."

217

I figured this guy had to be about my dad's age, which is Swing Era music, not rock. And on cruises, my dad's five piece group plays mostly GB. That's shorthand for "general business" music: a little of everything, pop, standards, wedding songs, and sneak in a couple jazz numbers. So I couldn't figure how his obvious connection to my dad's scene would bring him to a venue like this: a psychedelic rock, anti-war, "flower-power", flare bottoms, and "light shows" kind of happening.

"No offense," he whispered, "but you don't look too much like your Dad.

"No offense, but you don't look like you belong here," I said.

"I guess not. I just have an interest in 60's culture. Jack, you're the oldest, right?" Jim guessed. He's told me a lot about you two. Even mentioned your rope invention. Talked mostly about music and his kids. He's very proud of all his kids...and all his grandkids and the kids grandkids. You folks had a lot of kids!

Your dad and I were talking about that once, when he tried to guess how many diapers he's cleaned... the number he's changed while trying not to stick one of you in a vital organ with a diaper pin. That kinda led him to tell me about a diaper clasp he invented that was safer than pins because it grabbed the diaper edges and latched them together...nothing to stick into a baby's side, or worse, if it broke. He showed me one. It was a really solid design. When I saw and heard all that, I told him that the two of us meeting was quite a coincidence because I was the design engineer for the first disposable diaper! We heard of his diaper clasp, and it caused us to really step up getting our idea into production. Can you believe that?"

218

"No, I can't," I rasped, "I mean, that's too much, man. What did my father say? He never told me about meeting you-- the guy who, ah..." I trailed off.

"I know, don't feel bad to say it: My product beat his to the market. Our company and I made millions. His idea was made obsolete. And Eddie lost more than money. He lost the future he saw for you guys. I feel badly about that. But another group was right behind us with a plastic, snap diaper, so cloth was on the way out. Plastic was coming in...end of story. Anyway, your father asked me to look you up if I came to this part of Florida, and here I am. But I never thought I'd find you. You're not in the book. Then I saw this ad for a Hippie dance, and I figured, 'Why not try my luck at finding you there?' This is some good luck, just playing a hunch, and here you are. Plus, the glow ropes in action."

"Thanks for the kind words and praise, Jim. We're glad to meet you, too."

"They really get your attention-- very dynamic effect", Jim said, looking at the ropes on the table.

"We appreciate that. Can I buy you a drink?"

"No. Thank you. I'm fine with one drink."

"I'll tell my dad we ran into you. We had a great time," I said, hoping to get Carly ready for a polite departure, "Thanks for the drinks. What's your number, Jim? I'll give you a call if you're gonna be around here for a while."

"You're leaving? Hang on a minute, Jack. Before you go, I want to talk about the rope with you two. A little business talk."

219

"Like what kind of business, Jim?"

"Are you interested in selling me the rope?" he asked in a serious tone, "I have a son who wants to start a business in something fun from the 60's. He used to be a lawyer, but he became tired of that work. I think it's called "burn out". Doesn't do too much, lately. He often says he was the happiest in college during the 60's; wishes he was more a part of it. Guess that's why I've always got an eye and ear open for 60's stuff.

He's heard me talk about your rope from what your father described to me. Lately, he's seen young people in bars twirling glowing sticks. He thinks a more flexible, colorful "toy" like that would sell big with today's party generation and the "Back to the 60's" crowd. He'd love to have it."

"Well, sure, Jim. I can sell you this blue-green-purple one for ten bucks." He pushed a check over to us very slowly. [I hate taking checks, worrying whether they'll bounce. I'd rather give it away and feel good] "Actually, -- no charge, Jim. I'll put it on my dad's tab. It's yours. And please give our best to your son." I started to push the check back to Jim.

"Better take a look at that check you're sliding over to me before you put that much on your dad's tab," he said with a curious smile.

I turned the check around, and we just stared at it for a few seconds. The amount was so large, so unexpected, we couldn't directly respond to Jim's offer. All I could think was "Why?" I had no answer for him, only questions.

"Why would you want to pay us this much money

for the rights to our rope? How did you come up with this exact amount? Or is this a joke? I wouldn't appreciate that, Jim. Cuz' we've had our hearts broken before trying to finalize deals on this rope. Real deals, so it's not a source of laughs for us, man."

"Nothing funny here, Jack. It's a bonafide check for that amount. I would have brought a cashier's check if I knew you'd be here with the ropes... and they looked that good. I just never expected such luck."

I was having a hard time believing this could be for real. It was far easier to accept the possibility he was crazy or trying to scam us. But, he knew my dad's nickname; knows the size of my family; my name, and all about the diaper clasp, too, for cripes sake. So, he must know my father. I should call him. Get this Jim Fromme's whole story. Then see if we can do business.

But, Holy jeezus! What if he is for real? Am I supposed to haggle with him? And why should I? This is a lot of money; even after all the work, the rejection, and bad luck. We were looking at more than we ever expected for the glowers. I asked him if he wanted to check this out with his son first. He didn't. He was sure it was exactly the right project and the one his son wanted.

"And the offer I'm making easily fits within the research development budget. Our reason for making a large offer is this: we don't want to lose the chance to get a patent on a product that has old time "fad" potential. I'm in a position to know that the market for quality paraphernalia is going to take-off. I can see that I'm the first person to approach you with an offer in forty years. But I won't be the last. Sorry for the shock, Jack. Other interests are also looking for ready-to-go designs for all kinds of things."

221

"As much as we would like having all this money, I think you should give this to my dad if you're trying to settle..."

"I have no guilt about the past. I explained that. This money is a fair price for the past investment in work and trials you've put into these ropes. It's also a small price for what's left of my son's future. I want this product for him to develop; to have some fun making money in a relaxed way. And we will make money with your rope.

This check isn't for charity and it's certainly no joke. If you need a reason with your money, that's all I can offer. Or do you need more money?"

I looked at Carly, her pretty eyes all streaked in eyeliner. She looked to be in shock, but she just shrugged her shoulders. Then she said: "I don't want to see you make the wrong decision. I can't help you decide, though, because I can live with it, either way. You can't."

All I stood to lose was 50 bucks worth of Styrofoam, and a new black light. Oh... and the rights to a product that maybe someone else might be interested in buying at some unknown price. I still suspected it was all too good to be true, but I had to accept my good luck just like I had to accept the bad luck back in 1968. I suddenly heard myself saying:

"It's a generous offer, Jim. We gladly accept," grabbing his hand, shaking it in my shaking hands, "I'll call my nephew tomorrow to draw up the paperwork. But since the last deal I had suddenly collapsed, I'd feel even better if we could lock you in a safe room before an infamous Bay Area lightning bolt hits you before you can deposit the money in my account."

I called my dad that night and the next morning,

but I couldn't reach him. What would he do? I decided he'd go for it, but be prepared for a snag in the line. That would mean: "No celebrating until the money's in the bank".

Jim arrived at my condo in a taxi. I had the patent papers and the sales agreements ready for signature. All the ropes, except the original, were in a bag with the new black light. He had what he needed for the transaction— electronic money. I was so nervous I could barely sign the papers. Once the deposit cleared, I had to sit down. I never saw my bank account jump up $300,000.00 before. I needed to calm down.

"Let's go out for a few, Jim. We'll go over to Gulfport. Carly's buying!"

"Thanks for the offer, but I'll have to take a rain check, Jack. I've got a flight ready to take these ropes home. Oh, one thing, Jack. Call Show Biz and tell him there's another inventor in the family."

"I'll be sure to let him know about our deal, but I'm just a toy inventor, Jim. My father's the real inventor. You know that his invention was designed for something important...protecting babies. Only your plastic diaper could top his creation for safety. We all like to solve a problem, though. In that way, I suppose I am a kind of inventor.

So, good luck with the Glow Ropes. They've been like a member of this family. Now they're in your family. You should know that good pot helps with the effects but, for now, you can't sell that with the ropes."

"Why did I always know that, Jack? But laws can change."

We watched him drive away, feeling a happy numbness, knowing our world was about to change -- no more "working retirement" shit. Carly disappeared into the den. She came back carrying the old black bag we kept in the closet. It had our original glow rope in it, along with a scratched black light, yellowed E-Z Widers, and some wicked, aged pot in an old prescription bottle. She held the party bag out to me. I hadn't smoked in decades, but seeing all that money in our bank account made me feel like having a toke or two.

"Ready to party, old man?"

"Got matches, pretty lady?"

"Go West, young man!" was replaced with the mandate: "Get your college degree, buddy!" for this generation of parents and their Boomer brood. Veteran's benefits made it possible for the common man to become the college man, and these veterans were determined to secure this passageway to the High Life for themselves, their sons and daughters. So schools were built all over the suburbs to thank the veterans and produce some brainiacs who could devise more and better weapons to keep America safe. American society hyped intelligence and book learnin' to be as much a part of national defense as John Wayne's Seabee bulldozer. It became guardedly "ok" for boys to excel in school. Roger grew up during this brief window of sexy, manly intellectualism that has since been degraded to mass media's Nerdland.

While the iron was hot, young Roger struck. With full support and assistance from his parents, he was prodded and praised from one report card, skill mastery, and school level to another. His I.Q., when finally tested, was so high that the school wouldn't tell him or his family what it was. He only knew it was pretty damn high because he could pull off all kinds of shit and still get V.I.P. treatment from school authorities, while other clowns were pushed back a whole year and exiled to the educational gulag.

The author cruised along right through most of high school and college, until he suddenly found himself gutting it out through pot-induced disambition, coping with the sexual and emotional monsoons of teen marriage and fatherhood, and narrowly escaping the Draft, alcoholism, and total disillusionment. He emerged from the zenith of the 60's Counter-culture, drug culture, sexual revolution and alternative life style with degrees in Ancient History and Economics from Rhode Island College; and a Master's of Library Science from the University of Rhode Island. Along the way, he became Editor of The Outdoor Message, a statewide, environmental, monthly tabloid.

Finally forced out of blue collar jobs during the 70's Recession, he began a thirty year career with the emerging, multi-campus Community College of Rhode Island. He became a founding member of the state's Higher Education Library Information Network, a Full Professor of Information Science, a union agitator and the first Chairman of Library Faculty. He probably received his highest accolade when, his wavy hair and moustache having reached that perfect hint of grey, he became the unofficial Poster Professor for the College's media and in-house publications. He was proud to be succeeded in this hot and edgy position by his esteemed colleague, Wayne, the —Wizard of Chem Technology, and career guru to legions of single-parent mothers.

His hobbies included driving dangerously repaired sport cars, getting a tan, and travelling extensively throughout Rhode Island. Now he's done with those things, dabbling in photography of Bay Area beaches, birds, boats, and boobs. He resides in Tampa Bay area with the same 60's chick, only a toll booth away from the Gulf-side condos of their - wicked awesome son and daughter. He didn't write The High Life for himself, he wrote it for YOU. So, do the right thing and buy this book. It won't take long to read.

www.ingramcontent.com/pod-product-compliance
Lightning Source LLC
Chambersburg PA
CBHW030521100426
42813CB00001B/113